Praise for
The Secret of Inner Strength

"I found his superbly written autobiography as exciting and inspirational as he is."

—Priscilla Presley

"After reading Chuck Norris's remarkable autobiography, I know why he is and deserves to be a genuine folk hero."

—Roger Moore

"Plain-spoken . . . blends Norris's memories of his life with tips on how to cope with challenges and obstacles that face individuals on a day-to-day basis."

—*Gannett Newspapers*

"Amazingly candid and inspirational."

—*The Fighter*

"Meeting Chuck Norris changed my life, and reading his fascinating autobiography might change yours."

—Bob Barker

"Inspirational and motivational."

—*United Press International*

THE SECRET OF INNER STRENGTH

My Story

CHUCK NORRIS

WITH JOE HYAMS

CHARTER BOOKS, NEW YORK

This Charter Book contains the complete
text of the original hardcover edition.
It has been completely reset in a typeface
designed for easy reading, and was printed
from new film.

THE SECRET OF INNER STRENGTH: MY STORY

A Charter Book / published by arrangement with
Little, Brown and Company

PRINTING HISTORY
Little, Brown and Co. edition published 1988
Charter edition/March 1989

ISBN: 1-55773-175-6

Charter Books are published by The Berkley Publishing Group,
200 Madison Avenue, New York, New York 10016.
The name ''CHARTER'' and the ''C'' logo are trademarks
belonging to Charter Communications, Inc.

PRINTED IN THE UNITED STATES OF AMERICA

10 9 8 7 6 5 4 3 2 1

In memory of my brother Wieland, who was killed in Vietnam in June 1970, one month before his twenty-eighth birthday.

And to the three women in my life: to Granny Scarberry, who introduced me to the concept of inner strength; to my mother, Wilma, who taught me how to utilize that strength in my own life; and to my wife, Dianne, who has had the strength to put up with me for all these years.

THE SECRET OF INNER STRENGTH

INNER STRENGTH

My Story

PROLOGUE

PEOPLE SOMETIMES TELL me how lucky I have been in my life. When I hear that, I smile. Whatever luck I had, I made. I was never a natural athlete, but I paid my dues in sweat and concentration and took the time necessary to learn karate and become the world champion. I simply made up for what I lacked physically with work and determination. You get out of something what you put into it, and I've always been willing to give my all to whatever I do.

My mother taught me two valuable lessons. Despite hardships and problems that would have destroyed many people, she never allowed negative thoughts to enter her mind and dwelled instead only on positive thoughts; and she gave me as a gift the belief that I could do whatever I

1

wanted to do, if I truly believed in my mind I would achieve it.

I had a karate student with a severe case of osteomalacia. His bones were so soft that they broke easily, and we had to put pads all over his body to keep him from getting hurt. Every training session was agony for him, but he was determined and stayed with it. He tested for his black belt six times before he finally passed. I also know two dyslexic men who taught themselves to read; today both are important publishers.

If you think positively and persist long enough, the goal you have set for yourself will inevitably materialize. Bruce Lee, for example, had bad eyesight and one leg that was shorter than the other. But he had a mental image of what he wanted, and he became the quintessential martial artist and the first Chinese superstar in American films. Each step of his life was a progression toward his goal.

The wonderful thing about America is that you can start to succeed at any age and no matter where you come from, whether it's the Chicago ghetto or the Oklahoma prairies, where I was born. In this great country of ours, everyone has the opportunity to be anything he or she wants, regardless of the circumstances of birth or the level of education or even of natural ability. I have no sympathy for young people today who, complaining that they have no hope for the future, try to escape reality by using drugs.

I believe that everyone can attain a certain degree of success. The problem with many people is that when an opportunity appears they turn away because they fear the challenge; they are not secure enough to accept the chance, so they let it pass.

Everyone has something buried inside that can make him successful. The trick is to encourage that latent ability to surface and then to use it to get whatever it is that will make you happy. It's all based on mind control—learning to maximize your assets and minimize your weaknesses.

In my case, I started life with most of the deck stacked against me. My father gave me a role model to avoid. I was raised principally by women—my mother and grandmother—yet I became a world champion in a traditionally masculine sport. I was probably the shyest kid in every one of the half-dozen schools I attended, but today I am a film star. I have more material possessions, success, and happiness than I ever dreamed possible.

I didn't do it alone; no one ever does. I had good support: a loving mother, brothers, and stepfather, and a childhood sweetheart who is my wife of twenty-nine years and my best friend. The road was not easy, nor was it always fun. But it was always interesting and continuously challenging.

Now let me tell you my story and how I found the secret of inner strength.

ONE

NOTHING EVER CAME easy for me, not even being born. My mother, Wilma, was only eighteen and was in labor almost seventy-two hours when she had me. After such a hard delivery, she almost lost both me and her life. Finally, in the early hours of March 10, 1940, I weighed in at six pounds, eight ounces. I was a "blue baby," meaning that I didn't breathe immediately after being born. My father, Ray, who was in the delivery room at the hospital in Oklahoma along with both of my grandmothers, was so unnerved that he fainted. That was the pattern of his life: when the going got rough, he dropped out.

For the first five days of my life I was fed with an eyedropper. The doctors then discharged my mother and me. She took me to a friend's farm in Ryan, the small town we lived in on the border of Texas and Oklahoma. We stayed there until she got her strength back.

The name on my birth certificate is Carlos Ray Norris. My first name came from the Reverend Carlos Berry, my family's minister in Ryan. My middle name came from my father.

My parents were a handsome couple. Dad was about 6'1", well-built and strong, with coal-black hair and black eyes. In early photos he resembles John Wayne. Mom, who was just fifteen when they were married in Marietta, Oklahoma, was petite, with long, flowing red hair and freckles.

Genetically speaking, I am equal parts Irish and Indian. My paternal grandfather was Irish, while my paternal grandmother was a full-blooded Cherokee Indian. My mother's family name was Scarberry. My maternal grandmother, Agnes, was Irish, while my maternal grandfather was a Cherokee from Kentucky.

I inherited my light-brown hair and fair complexion from the Irish side of the family; I suspect that some of my stoicism in the face of adversity comes from the Indian branch. When I was fighting I used to tease those opponents I knew well by saying that if I couldn't beat them with my Irish temper, I would scalp them after the match.

We moved thirteen times before I was fifteen years old. As a child, I never knew what it was like to have real roots and a sense of community. All that moving around had an effect on me: once I started to earn a regular income I wanted to settle in. After we had lived for nearly two decades in our last home, my wife, Dianne, found anoth house and arranged the move herself; I protested all the way.

A few months after I was born, Granny Scarberry, a widow with two young daughters still at home, became ill. She needed my parents' help, so we moved to her house in Wilson, Oklahoma. Dad, who was a mechanic, got a job with a car dealer. When Granny was well again we moved to Lawton, Oklahoma, where Dad drove a Greyhound bus. Although I was only an infant at the time, I can remember him taking me along once on his route. Another vivid memory I have of that period is of being carried on Dad's shoulders as he strung fishing lines across the Red River in Oklahoma. It's sad, but those are two of my best child-hood memories of him. When World War II broke out, Dad had a choice of either being drafted or working in a defense plant. His brother lived in Richmond, California, so he went there and got a job in the shipyards. Mom, who was pregnant again, took me back to her mother's house in Wilson. Toward the end of her pregnancy, she realized that she wanted Dad with her when she gave birth. So the two of us went by train to California.

We moved into a small apartment in a building that only housed defense workers. My brother Wieland was born there on July 12, 1943. A few months later Dad was drafted into the Army, and Mom took Wieland and me back to Granny Scarberry's.

Wilson was a very small prairie town, flat, dusty, and arid. It had a population of about five thousand, mostly elderly retired folk. We lived in a small clapboard house on a tiny patch of land. Wieland, Mom, and I slept in one room. I shared a pallet on the floor with my brother, and we were bathed together in a big galvanized tin washtub. Our toilet was an outhouse. When I was old enough, I used to walk the two miles to my aunt's house to use her facilities because I hated that outhouse so much.

One day Mom received a telegram: Dad was missing in action. I was too young to know what that meant, except that he might not be coming home. But the two strong, consistent forces in my life were my mother and Granny Scarberry, and as long as they were around I felt safe.

We heard nothing else for three months. By the time we learned that Dad had been wounded, he was already home. He'd seen a lot of action, and when he returned to us he had a bad leg and a drinking problem.

When Dad was gone, we were happy and things were good. But when he came back, there was tension in the house. That was to become a repetitive pattern in my young life. My father was a good man when sober, but when he got drunk, which was often, little things like the water running when he was trying to sleep would send him into a tirade. He'd shout and make threats. Fortunately he never abused any of us physically—even when drunk he wasn't aggressive. For example, he never spanked me, but he did scold me. I was overly sensitive, and when he bawled me out I'd start to cry. When that happened he would pick me up in his arms, lie down on the bed with me, and apologize. If my mother spanked me, he'd say,

"I'm leaving." Now I realize that he simply could never stand confrontation. That was part of his drinking problem: he never faced up to the fact that he was an alcoholic, which would have been the first step in curing himself.

When I was six years old, we moved to Napa, California, where we had family. Dad went back to work at a Navy shipyard, and I started school. But Wieland had such bad asthma that we were forced to move again, this time to Miami, Arizona, where the climate was drier. We lived in a small cottage next to a gas station, and I was enrolled in the second grade.

Two things from that period stand out in my memory. One was the fact that most of the students in my school were Indians; the other was an Indian boy named Bobby who lived next door to us. He was my age but a lot larger and a real bully. For some reason or other, Bobby had it in for me and chased me home from school every day.

One day he broke a desk during recess, and the teacher accused me of being the culprit. In those days teachers spanked students. She announced that she was going to swat me. I knew that Bobby had done it, but I wasn't about to tell. I stood up and was following her into the hallway to get my swats when one of the other kids spoke up and said that I hadn't done it. I was off the hook. But Bobby still chased me home.

Jack, the man who owned the gas station and the cottages, couldn't stand to see me bullied. He told Mom he was going to make me fight Bobby. He insisted that she stay in the apartment and not interfere. That day, as I was running home, Jack stopped me and made me wait for Bobby.

"You're going to stand up for yourself and fight this kid right now," Jack said.

"He's too big," I said.

But Jack made me stand my ground. He fired me up. By the time Bobby arrived I was so mad that I wrestled him to the ground. I was getting the worst of it, however, until I got him by the finger. Bobby began to cry. "Give up?" I asked him. "I give," he said. I let go of his finger. He immediately jumped me again. I grabbed his finger again and began bending it back. Once more he started to cry. This time he really gave up.

Bobby never chased me again. In fact, we even became friends.

My behavior in this instance was to serve as a model for the characters I would play many years later in films: I accepted provocation until I couldn't handle it any longer, and then I fought back.

The move to Arizona didn't help Wieland's asthma; in fact, it got worse. So we packed up again and went back to Granny Scarberry's. Soon after the school year ended we moved once more, to Cyril, Oklahoma, where Dad had a job as a truck driver and Mom went to work as a waitress. We lived in a small hotel next door to the restaurant.

I still vividly remember the night Dad came home drunk and announced, "We're leaving. Get packed." We had to sneak out of the apartment because he hadn't paid the rent.

Mom made a bed for Wieland and me on top of the clothes stacked in the back seat of the car. Although Dad was drunk, he insisted on driving back to Wilson and Granny Scarberry's; Mom cried hysterically because she thought he was going to kill us all.

I've often wondered why Mom didn't leave him. I suspect she felt guilty because of what he had gone through during the war; I also believe she probably thought that a part-time father was better than no father at all.

Dad left again soon after that, this time for Hawthorne, California, where he got a job with Bethlehem Steel. Meanwhile, Mom got a job in Wilson as manager of a laundry. The move was just fine with me. I was always happy at Granny Scarberry's home. She was a tiny woman with bright-blue laughing eyes who was always fun to be with, and she showered my brother and me with affection and attention. Wieland and I had lunch every day at the café next door to the laundry where Mom worked. It was a treat for us to eat there; at home we ate whatever was on the table, but in the restaurant we had a choice of anything on the menu.

I used to patrol the streets of Wilson every day after school and collect pop bottles that I would return to the grocery for a refund. I also picked up scrap iron that I sold for a penny a pound.

There was one movie theater in Wilson where for a dime I could spend all Saturday afternoon watching the double feature and the serials. I loved those Saturdays. With a nickel bag of popcorn on my lap, I could escape into another world. I went to Casablanca with Humphrey Bogart; Cary Grant took me to India. My favorite movies were Westerns, especially the ones with John Wayne. For those few hours in the movie theater when I watched a John Wayne movie, I *became* him.

Like most kids my age, I dreamed of becoming a cowboy. I remember seeing a toy gun in a store window and wanting it more than anything else in the world. But my mother couldn't afford it. It was a big disappointment to me, and she knew it, but she said there would be many things in life that I would not be able to have when I wanted them, and I should think of them as goals to be achieved. If I kept the goal in mind, accepting the fact that there would be setbacks and obstacles, and continued to work toward succeeding, one day I would reach that goal. That was pretty heady stuff for a kid to understand, but some of it sank in. Much, much later it was to become an integral part of my own philosophy.

Boys who have no strong male role models in their childhood often tend to grow up confused. My father was a role model in reverse—a model to avoid. But my mother had such a loving and caring nature that she more than made up for his shortcomings. She never let herself get down or depressed; no matter how bad things were, she stayed up. Even though we had a hard life, she still maintained the attitude that everything was fine. She took life one day at a time, made the best of every day, and never let things get the better of her. I remember her coming home exhausted from her job at the laundry and saying that we were lucky—that as bad as things seemed to be, there were people far worse off than we were. She never expounded "positive thinking," at least not in the way that is popular today, but her example was enough to set me on the road to right thinking. She was the most positive influence in my life, and she taught my brother and me to never think of the bad, but only of the good, and to do what had to be done without complaint. That philosophy of hers became an integral part of my life and the core of my inner strength.

Since I didn't have real toys to play with, I used clothespins. They were my soldiers or cowboys. In my stash I had large pins and small ones. I always made the big ones the bad guys and the little ones the good guys.

I used to play in the dirt in our front yard. I'd set up my cast of characters and prepare for the battle. I'd hide the big pins behind a rock or tree stump and then I would have the little pins jump in and do battle. I'd visualize the fight in my mind and decide what each pin was going to do, and then I'd start the battle. Years later, when I became a karate fighter, I used the same technique of visualization before each bout.

I have never been psychoanalyzed, but I believe that even at that early age I subconsciously wanted to be mentally, psychologically, and emotionally strong. I believe you can determine your destiny in life by planting the proper seed. If you feed it and nourish it, sooner or later it will bear fruit.

If I were to be psychoanalyzed, I am certain that one painful incident that took place when I was eight years old would come up for examination. My cousin Dean, who was about my age, went with me occasionally to visit a neighbor's house. One day, when we were alone in the house, we saw a bottle full of change. On an impulse, we took it. Of course, the neighbors missed the money instantly and mentioned the loss to my mother. Mom asked me whether I knew anything about it. I was never a good liar and tried to avoid answering. She knew by the look on my face that I was guilty. Finally I admitted that I had stolen the money, but I said nothing about Dean's involvement.

Mom told me to go get the money and return it. I was mortified, but I did it. To make matters worse, the neighbors said, ''We didn't think a nice boy like you would do a thing like that.''

This episode taught me a lesson. I did steal, and I had to face it. The confrontation was a horrible experience that I never wanted to go through again. Mom said I learned a good lesson, and, as always, she was right.

In November 1949, Mom took us on the train to join Dad in Hawthorne, California. The four of us moved into a twenty-foot house trailer shaped like a teardrop. It was parked next door to my Aunt Gladys's home. The trailer was so small that Wieland and I had to share the same bed. At night, before we said our prayers and she put us to bed, Mom would sing ''Dear Hearts and Gentle People'' with us.

There was a country-Western bar with a band near our house, and Dad used to hang out there. He occasionally took Wieland and me with him when Mom was working. We amused ourselves as best we could while he sat and drank with his buddies.

One night he dressed me up in cowboy boots and hat and told the bandleader that I knew a song. Before I was even aware of it, I was on stage singing. I don't remember the reaction I got, but I must have been terrible because Wieland was so embarrassed for me that he disappeared. We finally found him hiding under the shuffleboard near the jukebox. It was my first professional appearance, but it was soon to be followed by another.

A man came into the classroom of my elementary school and said he was looking for two boys and two girls in our class who could square-dance. Finally he came over to me and my cousin Jerry. Pointing at us, he said, "You two. Stand up."

For an hour every day after school Jerry and I and two girls took square-dancing lessons. After a few weeks of lessons our little group toured the Los Angeles area, putting on exhibitions before various social groups such as the Rotary Club. We weren't paid, but it was fun because we were all friends. The producers of the Doyle O'Dell television show heard of us and invited us to perform on the air. I remember very little about the show other than the fact that it was exciting and I had a new outfit to wear.

In March 1951, Mom became pregnant again. Once more, Dad took off. "You'll see," she told Wieland and me. "Things will get better when he comes back." Although I was only eleven years old, I knew better—nothing would change.

Mom moved us into the only shack in a nice neighborhood in Gardena, California. Mom wasn't able to work, so we had to go on welfare. Our only other income came from Dad's thirty-dollar-a-month government disability check—just enough to cover the rent.

Mom accepted things as they were and was determined to make the best of the situation. Her love and devotion for Wieland and me made our lack of material possessions seem insignificant. There were only the three of us, and we clung to each other. We didn't have a lot of clothes or toys, but Mom always made sure we had enough to eat. In fact, in those days I judged how well-off people were by how much they had to eat.

I was once invited over to a friend's home for dinner. They lived in a nice house, but when we sat down to eat there wasn't much on the table. When I came home I said to Mom, "Those poor people, they have hardly enough to eat."

Even today, if I were given a choice between having wealth and no love at home or having love at home and no wealth, I would want it just the way I had it. I grew up poor in material things but rich in love, and that, to me, is the key to a happy childhood.

Mom was not a gregarious person, but she was warm and friendly. She would meet someone—anyone—and within ten minutes they would be the best of friends. That openness is a wonderful gift. I don't have it, and I've always envied people who do.

Since my father was never around long enough to teach me physical things or to play games with me, I didn't excel at any competitive sport. Mom did her best as a substitute, throwing a ball with me in the lot behind our house, but it wasn't the same. She and my grandmother were overly protective of me, and I hadn't enough confidence in my own abilities to really try anything physically demanding.

In school I was shy and inhibited. When I knew that a teacher was going to call on me to recite something aloud in front of the class, I usually found an excuse to be absent. I can't explain why I was so shy; it just seemed to be my nature. Wieland, however, had inherited my mother's nature. Even as a child he was outgoing and fun-loving. People just naturally warmed to him, as he did to them.

My brother Aaron was born in November 1951. When he was about ten months old, Mom got a job at Northrop Aircraft as a silkscreen printer. She worked the three-to-midnight shift. Since we couldn't afford a baby-sitter, I had to rush home from school to baby-sit Wieland and Aaron, both of whom would start crying the moment Mom left for work.

The first night Mom went to work, Aaron was very temperamental. I finally figured out that if I rocked him he would settle down. When Mom came home she found me out by the road rocking him in my arms. I don't recall how

17

many hours I spent in a rocking chair holding my brother, but I didn't mind the baby-sitting chore. Mom had instilled in me the notion of assuming responsibility, and it seemed the natural thing to do.

Despite our hard times, we had a lot of fun. Our house was always full of laughter. Every morning on their way to school my friends would come by for a cup of hot chocolate. On weekends there was always an impromptu ball game in our back yard. Mom liked to make ice cream. We couldn't afford a television set, so she would make a game of wrapping us in a blanket and then would sit with us on the bed while we ate ice cream and listened to mystery programs such as *Inner Sanctum* on the radio.

Even though Mom had only a ninth-grade education herself, she was very smart. Before she went to work at night she would sit and help me with my homework. In fact, we learned algebra together.

Then Dad returned home, and the fun times ceased. He got a job as a mechanic at a gas station. On weekends I would go there to help out and pump gas. I have never been mechanically skilled; even today my wife changes the light bulbs in our house. Dad was impatient with me because I didn't show any flair for working with my hands.

He was still drinking. He pawned the bicycle Mom had bought me for Christmas, which I rode to school. Every week or so he would pawn our record player for five dollars. Mom would go to the pawnshop on payday and get it back. Before going to sleep at night I used to pray

18

for things to get better, for Dad to quit drinking and become a better father.

One night Dad had a bad car accident and was arrested for drunk driving. He was sentenced to a road camp for six months. Mom took me out to see him on weekends a few times. He looked great and seemed to be in good health. The hard work agreed with him, and we prayed that when he got released he might be off the liquor for good—he hadn't had a drink for six months. But the moment he came home, he went straight back to the bar.

Many years later, when I was having financial problems, something came up between my wife, Dianne, and me. I told Dianne to get in the car. We drove to Gardena and parked in front of that shack. "I had to live there when I was young," I told Dianne. "I'll never have to go back to that kind of life if I'm willing to put forth the effort to achieve the level of success I have set for myself."

The year I was fifteen we moved to a slightly better house in Torrance, California. Dad, who had taken off again, returned with an even worse drinking problem. For the first time he was becoming aggressive at home and abusive toward Mom. He would come home drunk and wake Mom and me up in the middle of the night and make us walk to a liquor store to buy a bottle for him. We didn't have a car, and I remember it was a long walk to the nearest store.

Because Dad was drunk most of the time, I was embarrassed to have friends come to the house. I never knew what shape he would be in. I was dating a girl who said she wanted to meet my parents. Rather than bring her home, I broke up with her.

Dad was so handsome that women would actually walk up and flirt with him in front of Mom. I think she was able to handle his womanizing, but she couldn't take his drinking. I was just sixteen when, after my brothers were asleep, Mom and I talked about what she should do. We finally agreed that it was silly to continue living on the razor's edge of uncertainty with him, never knowing when he would leave or come home or what shape he would be in or how he would behave. She finally decided that it would be better for all of us if she got a divorce.

It was about this time that one of those things happened that you don't think much of at the time but later recall vividly: Wieland told Mom that he wouldn't live to be twenty-eight years old. Mom laughed at this and told him it was nonsense-thinking, that all children have such fantasies. But the conversation troubled her, so much so that she told me about it. I reacted the same way Mom had. I scoffed at the crazy premonition and put it out of my mind.

My parents were divorced in 1956. I was sixteen, Wieland was twelve, and Aaron was just four. A year later Mom met George Knight, a foreman at Northrop, where she worked. George was a very gentle man who genuinely cared for her. She told me that he had asked her to marry him, and she asked for my opinion. I thought George would be a fine husband. Soon after our conversation, they were married.

Although George had three kids of his own, he treated us as though we were all one family. For the first time in my life I had a strong family support system. George took over responsibility for all of us, which gave me the opportunity to be a real teenager. I started to come out of my shell and make friends. With George's encouragement, I became interested in sports. I went out for the football team and made the second string. I even joined a car club called The Senators. School wasn't easy for me, but I worked extra hard and wound up making good grades.

I discovered a new pride in myself and began to blossom thanks to family unity and a strong paternal influence. I finally had a father who could serve as a role model. As a result, I have always been there for my sons and tried to make certain that they know they can depend on me and that I care.

One day when I came home from high school I found my real father in the living room of the house. Mom was crying. "What are you doing here?" I asked him.

"I'm waiting for George," he said.

"Why?" I asked.

"I'm going to take care of him."

His meaning was all too clear to me. "No, you're not," I said. "You're not going to touch him."

My father glared at me. "How do you plan to stop me?"

We went out into the front yard and squared off, leaving Mom inside the house frantically telephoning the police.

I had been afraid of my father all my life, and I was still afraid of him. I didn't know whether I could handle the situation, but I wasn't going to let him do anything to my stepfather.

I don't know whether my father saw fear in my eyes or determination, but he looked at me for a second, and a change came over him. "I'm not going to fight with you," he said, and he got into his car and drove off.

That was one of the last times I saw him.

I transferred from Gardena High to North Torrance High in the middle of my junior year. I was still shy, however. I never got up and talked in front of a class because I was certain that I would say the wrong thing and turn red all over, as I always did when I became embarrassed.

As I was going to class one day, my cousin Jo-Ellen pointed out a blonde who I thought was one of the prettiest girls in school. Her name was Dianne Holechek. Jo-Ellen said Dianne had told her that I was the man she was going to marry. I was flabbergasted and thought Jo-Ellen was putting me on.

But it seemed to me that wherever I went, Dianne was also there. At the time, I was working after school as a box boy in Boy's Market. I still remember the night I was going down an aisle and saw Dianne coming toward me. I was surprised because I knew she didn't live near the market. She asked me where the bread was. We faced each other in embarrassed silence for a long moment. Finally I turned red and pointed.

A few days later I saw Dianne walking in front of me across campus after school. I asked whether I could drive her home. I had a beat-up old Dodge that I had bought for $150. It was so ugly that I parked it blocks away from school so no one would see it, but Dianne didn't seem to care. Before dropping her off, I asked whether she would like to go to a movie with me on the weekend. She smiled, and we made a date.

George lent me his beautiful blue '51 Ford for the occasion, and I took Dianne to a drive-in movie. We held hands during the show. When I brought her home, I parked and tried to kiss her. Dianne told me we didn't know each other well enough. She didn't slap my face, however, so I asked her out again. After our fourth date she invited me to her home to have dinner with her family. Her father worked in the aircraft industry, and she had an older sister and two brothers. They were all very outspoken and loved to tease each other; I doubt I said one word during the whole meal. I don't know whether I passed their test, but I survived it.

I guess it's true that opposites attract, because Dianne was everything I wasn't. She was outgoing and self-assured; I was shy and insecure. She wasn't the studious type; I had to keep at the books to get good grades. And she was popular, while I doubt that most of the kids in the class knew anything about me. But she chased me until I caught her. We went steady all through my last year of high school. I even bought her a tiny diamond engagement ring on the installment plan. You needed a magnifying glass to see it. Over the twenty-nine years we have been married, I have given her a lot of expensive jewelry, but I doubt that any gift brought her more joy than that simple ring.

One day George handed me the keys to his new car and said he was going to trade with me. He drove my old Dodge to work so I would have a nice car for my last year at school. Not many fathers, real or adoptive, would have done that. I have never forgotten that gesture, which was so typical of the man I am proud to call Pop.

High school kids had pretty innocent pleasures in those days, and social drinking was one of them. I never drank, however, probably because I had seen what it had done to my father. One night Dianne and I went with a group of friends to a party. As a joke, we decided to get one of the girls drunk. Someone bought a bottle of cheap Thunderbird wine, but the girl refused to touch it. "If it's so good, why don't you have some, Carlos?" she said. I took a drink to prove that it was fine. Hey, I thought, this stuff isn't so bad. I took another swallow and ended up drinking the whole bottle.

I don't have a clear memory of the rest of the night; I do know that Dianne drove me home, stopping now and then to allow me to throw up. When I finally made it into bed I was moaning. I heard Mom tell George, "Carlos is sick." George looked in on me and reported, "He's sick, all right."

The next morning George woke me early. "I want you to paint the garage," he said. The hangover plus the smell of paint darn near killed me.

24

Two weeks later, while I was working at the market, someone broke a bottle of wine in an aisle. I was told to clean it up. The smell of the wine started me gagging again. To this day I can't stand the smell of cheap wine; in fact, I rarely drink at all except for an occasional beer or an iced tea with a shot of Grand Marnier (a Chuck Norris Kicker).

Shortly before graduation I went with five other members of the football team to have a few beers at an amusement park in Long Beach called The Pike. After the beers we looked around for something to do. As fate would have it, there was a tattoo parlor nearby. One of the fellows said, "Let's go get a tattoo." We walked in, and the proprietor asked, "Who's going to be first?" We all looked at each other. Finally I volunteered.

I sat in the chair, and he asked me what I wanted. "I don't know," I said.

"I can't tattoo you unless you tell me what you want," he responded.

I thought a moment. "How about my girlfriend's name?"

"Great," he said. "Where do you want it?"

I rolled up the sleeve on my left arm and told him I wanted *Dianne,* with two *n*'s.

He shaved my left forearm and started to work. I tried not to show the pain even as blood flowed all over. After he finished, he looked at my friends and asked, "Who's next?" Almost in unison they said, "Not me." We left. I was the only one to get tattooed.

It's a good thing Dianne and I got married. There

25

just aren't that many Diannes with two *n*'s around.

After graduation I wanted to join the police department, but I was too young. I figured that if I went into the Air Force I could get into the Military Police and gain some experience in police work. In August 1958 I enlisted and was sent to boot camp at Lackland Air Force Base in Texas.

During boot camp one of my barrack mates asked me what Carlos meant in English. I told him it was the same as Charles. "Then we'll call you Chuck," he said. The nickname stuck, although my family, wife, and old friends still call me Carlos.

I wrote almost daily to Dianne and waited impatiently for her letters, which frequently crossed mine in the post. I proposed to her in a letter, and her *Yes* came back by return mail.

Dianne made all the wedding arrangements. When I came home on leave in December we were married in church in a simple Episcopalian ceremony attended by our families. I wore my uniform. Dianne looked radiant in a white gown. My brother Wieland, who was my best man, rented a tux for the occasion. I was eighteen, and Dianne had just turned seventeen and was still in high school.

I was earning only eighty-four dollars a month in the military and had no money for a honeymoon. I had to borrow from Dianne's father to pay for our four-day honeymoon in Big Bear, California.

Dianne quit school to go with me to my first base in Gila Bend, Arizona. We lived off base in a twelve-foot-long trailer with no bathroom; we had to use the community shower. One pitch-black night, Dianne and I went to the shower together. As we were walking back to our trailer, gravel suddenly came flying at our feet and a black figure ran right at us. Dianne screamed, jumped behind me, and unintentionally pinned my arms to my sides. The dark figure came running right at us. I'm dead, I thought. However, the ''assailant'' turned out to be our neighbor playing a joke on us. Later I wondered what I would have done had it really been someone intent on harming us. That thought was to trouble me many times after the incident.

Since we couldn't afford a car, I hitchhiked to the base every day and Dianne walked to her waitress job at a Dairy Queen ice cream stand. We lived in the trailer for about three months before moving into a small apartment, our first real home together. I bought a battered old '51 Studebaker for $150, and Dianne then drove me to and from the base.

We were only kids, and it wasn't easy for either of us to adjust to married life, but we had one thing going for us: when we got into an argument, Dianne couldn't go home to her mother because she didn't have the money!

The base at Gila Bend was really a gunnery range where pilots from Luke Air Force Base in Phoenix practiced war games. I was assigned to the Military Police. One of our jobs was to seal off the perimeter of crash sites. There were frequent crashes because it was so hot that the jets on the T33 trainers would flame out.

After a particularly bad crash, one of the ground crew picked up a helmet. The pilot's head was still in it! No one knew it until the crewman keeled over in a dead faint.

Sometimes I was assigned to escort visiting senior officers around the base. I took the job seriously and maintained a discreet and respectful attitude. My partner was just the opposite. He was an outgoing young man who had no hesitation about striking up a conversation with an officer and being friendly. I didn't have that kind of self-confidence. I was an Airman Third Class and had accumulated the time in grade for a promotion to Airman Second Class. But when rank time came up my partner was promoted and I wasn't. When I got passed over for promotion, I knew I was doing something wrong.

As a newlywed who looked forward to having a family, I realized that if I was going to get ahead in this world I needed to change my attitude and personality so people wouldn't get promoted over me all the time. I realized that I couldn't just sit back hoping for the breaks to come my way, because they don't happen by hoping—they happen because of positive actions. But knowing that you have to change and knowing *how* to change are two different things.

We had been living in the apartment for about a year when I was sent on an isolated tour (i.e., without family) to Korea. Dianne went back to her parents' home in Torrance. She got a job as a checker in a grocery store and went to night school to earn her high school diploma.

I had no way of knowing it then, but my stint in Korea was to become the major turning point in my life.

It is important to have a goal in mind. Accept the fact that there will be setbacks and obstacles. But if you continue to visualize that goal and work toward it, one day you will achieve it.

Do what has to be done without complaint and think only positively. Don't allow yourself to think negatively.

TWO

WHEN I ARRIVED at Osan Air Base in Korea, I found that there were four things I could do with my spare time: (1) hang around the barracks and play cards, (2) booze it up, (3) enroll in an academic class, or (4) study the martial arts. Judo was the only martial art I had heard of, so I joined the judo club on the base. I had never learned any basic defensive skills and was not confident in my ability to handle a crisis, but I didn't want to spend my life worrying about the possibility of one.

A troublesome situation had occurred one night at Gila Bend just before I left for Korea. While on base patrol, I got a call for assistance: a drunk sergeant was causing a ruckus at the NCO Club. When I arrived there I saw a mountain of a man tearing the place apart. I went over to him and said, "OK, Sarge, let's cut it out." Suddenly he grabbed me by the shirt and threw me across the room. I had no intention of drawing my .45, and I didn't think my billy club was going to do much good. While I was considering my next move, the MP sergeant, a big man himself, came in and resolved the situation before someone got hurt—most probably me.

During my first two weeks of judo training, I became ill with diarrhea, probably from drinking the local water. Most of the soldiers I had come overseas with had already finished their bouts with the illness. I was determined to avoid it by imbibing only soft drinks. When I started training in judo, however, I perspired a lot and needed water to keep from dehydrating. I finally took the plunge. Literally. My barrack mates kidded me unmercifully as I dashed back and forth between the barracks and the latrine.

As luck would have it, just as I was getting well I broke my shoulder in an awkward fall to the judo mat. On the other hand, maybe it was good luck that it happened when it did—it would've been a bear to run to the latrine every few minutes with my shoulder taped up.

A few days after my accident, I went for a walk at dinnertime through the village of Osan with its straw huts and shabby market stalls. The aroma of *kimchi* (cabbage cooked with garlic) was almost overpowering in the narrow alleys. On the outskirts of Osan, I heard fierce yelling and saw people's heads popping up over the top of a hill. Curious, I walked up the hill to see what was going on. Several Koreans in white *gis* (martial-arts uniforms) were jumping up in the air and executing spectacular kicks. I had done some gymnastics in high school, but I hadn't known that the human body was capable of such amazing feats. I wanted to ask them what they were doing, but I was apprehensive about interrupting them.

When I returned to the base I told my judo instructor, Mr. Ahn, what I had seen. I asked if he knew what it was. He told me that it was a style of Korean karate called tang soo do, the art of empty-hand fighting, utilizing feet and hands as weapons. In those days, karate was only a word to me. I asked Mr. Ahn what he thought about my training in karate until my shoulder healed. He said it might be a good idea and introduced me to Mr. Jae Chul Shin, the chief instructor. There weren't many Americans training in martial arts in Korea at that time, and we had a sorry reputation for not sticking with it. But thanks to Mr. Ahn's recommendation I was accepted as a student.

Mr. Shin gave lessons outside on the hard ground, in an area walled in by bamboo fences. There were twenty students, most of them Korean black belts, with only a few Americans. Everyone, including the beginners, just jumped right into the class and tried to struggle along. The theory was that if you wanted to learn, you learned, but no one actively encouraged you. The Koreans were not into the psychology of teaching. The other students were indifferent to me, and I did my best to keep up with them.

During the first few weeks of training on the hard ground I had a problem with my feet, which had always been tender. When I was an infant and my mother didn't want me to run around, she would take off my shoes and put me in the front yard. She knew I wouldn't get up and walk. I don't know why my feet were so sensitive; they just were. It took time for them to toughen up.

The daily training sessions were five hours long, Monday through Saturday. I was not limber, and the stretching exercises we had to do before each class were pure agony for me. Classes started at 5:00 P.M., when I finished my duties at the base, and ended at 10:00 P.M., with five minutes' rest between each hour.

For the first twenty minutes of each day's session we warmed up by punching from a wide stationary stance. Then we practiced blocking punches for forty minutes. For the next hour we practiced the different kicks: front, side, round, and back. We spent the third hour working in pairs, with one partner blocking and countering the other's punches or kicks with kicks or punches of his own; then we reversed the procedure, with the partner who had earlier attacked now doing the blocking and countering. We ended the hour with those flying kicks in the air that I had first admired. For the fourth hour we did *heians*,* choreographed movements fighting an imaginary opponent. During the final hour we free-sparred or fought against each other without making contact. It was the same routine day in and day out. It never varied, and it was especially difficult for me since I had only one good arm and no one

---

*In some sections of this book I have used Japanese words rather than their Korean equivalents because I believe the former may be more familiar to readers.

was any easier on me because of my injury. Also, I was not in particularly good physical shape, nor was I especially well coordinated. Actually, the fact that I was on such a low physical level probably worked to my advantage. As a teacher myself, I have found that pupils who start with less natural physical ability are often more determined to develop, whereas students with tremendous ability often don't have the desire to achieve. That's why I never get excited about someone who is extremely well coordinated. I much prefer the more determined student.

After my arm healed, I continued to study judo for four hours every Sunday, my one day off from karate.

There were many nights when I went to bed so stiff and sore that I had to sleep on my back. But subconsciously I had been looking for a way to change. I felt that would happen with karate. Despite the agony of training, I said to myself, "If I can stick with this, I can stick with anything." I was learning discipline by developing the ability to do something that was never easy, not always pleasant, and about which I was not always enthusiastic. I had not set my mind on achieving any particular goal, such as becoming a black belt. And I had no inkling that karate would one day become the focal point of my life or that in eight years I would become the world champion.

Korea basically has three different climates: hot, cold, and rainy. For good reason, it's known both as one of the hottest places in the world and as one of the coldest. The summer temperature can soar to over 100°, with one-hundred-percent humidity. When it gets cold it also rains, and icy winds knife through Arctic gear. There's just no way to get warm.

In bad weather we trained in a Quonset hut. Training wasn't so bad when it was cold, because all that exercise built up body heat. During the hot weather we trained outdoors, but the air was so humid that within weeks I came down with a rash known as the Korean Krud. The flesh started peeling off my thighs from the humidity and from the friction of my legs when I worked out. I had to go to the hospital for three days until it was cured.

Meanwhile, I had my hands full with my job as an Air Force Policeman. The Koreans were resourceful people and had managed to hook up the electricity for the entire village of Osan by tapping into a wire from our base. Every night the village would light up. Occasionally I drew the late shift, and it was my duty to drive around the perimeter of the base and locate the connection. I'd find and remove the wires. The village would go totally dark. By the time I returned to HQ to report, however, the village would be ablaze with lights again.

One of my daytime jobs was to guard the main gate and check the Korean workers as they left, since government property was constantly being liberated. One day a *mamasan* (elderly woman) who must have been seventy years old approached the gate carrying a big bale of hay on her back. Before going through she sat on a curb to rest. I noticed that when she tried to get up, she couldn't. I went over to help her but was unable to heft the load. I started digging through the hay. An entire Jeep engine was hidden inside the bale. I confiscated it but soon regretted it—we had a terrible time hauling it back.

It took time for the Korean black belts to accept me, but when they saw how determined I was to learn they became more friendly. Part of my enthusiasm for karate was due to the fact that it was one of the few sports in which the only person you compete against is yourself. Soon I became one of Mr. Shin's most dedicated students.

In Korean karate a lot of emphasis was placed on toughening up the hands in order to be able to break boards and bricks, the theory at that time being that if you could hit hard enough to break a solid object, you could certainly damage an opponent. To strengthen my hands I used to carry a rock with me at all times. I held it in one hand and beat on it with my other fist to get and keep calluses on the knuckles.

When I was in my third month of training, Mr. Shin announced that we were going to put on a demonstration in the village of Osan. Toward the end of the demonstration he stacked up eight roofing tiles. He looked around at our group. "You," he said, pointing to me. "You break!" I felt my heart suddenly banging against my chest. I was honored that Mr. Shin had chosen me even though I'd never broken anything before, and I knew he would lose face in front of the villagers if I refused. I'd seen black belts break bricks, so I crouched over the tiles as they had and lined up my two knuckles on the top of the stack. I took a deep breath, exhaled, and went for it. But as my hand came down I twisted my wrist, and the small knuckles in my hand took the force of the blow. The pain was horrendous; my hand was broken. Mr. Shin had no comment. That was the Korean way of teaching: the student learned through trial and error.

Soon after my hand was out of the cast, I went into the village with a friend for a few beers. My friend got drunk and started an altercation with one of the waitresses. I thought he was going to hit her, so I grabbed him and told him to cool down. He spun around and hit me flush in the nose. We started fighting, and I punched him. That didn't faze him, so I kicked him. He dropped. I was astounded. The kicks I had been practicing really were effective! But he had broken my nose and I had rebroken my hand, which had to be put back into a cast.

I wrote to Dianne daily, telling her about my training. She apparently mentioned it to a police officer who shopped in the market where she worked. He was horrified. "My God, have him stop studying karate," he said. "He'll come home a killer." Dianne wrote and told me, "Stop taking that stuff." But by that time I had been promoted to red belt (a level just below black belt) and had no intention of quitting.

I had developed a certain amount of ability and began to enjoy it. I no longer got sore and stiff, and I was fascinated with the kicks, especially the spinning back kick, which I was finally perfecting.

For that kick, which would eventually become my trademark, I had to learn to face my opponent and then turn my back to him at the same time my foot shot out. The power came from a backward snap of the hips; the leg was bent until contact was made, and then it straightened out. In the beginning this was a difficult kick for me because it took more balance and coordination than a front kick.

Part of the power of the kick came from the mind. It was the mind that synchronized the spinning of the body, the pivoting of the hips, and the thrusting of the leg. The mind caused the air to be forced out of the lungs and the muscles of the abdomen and leg to tense on contact.

As I got into better shape, I was beginning to feel better about myself, because I was training both body and mind. The fact that for the first time in my life I had stuck with something and had not given up brought about mental development. That combination of discipline and learning led to confidence, a stage of inner strength.

It took about six months, but as I became more proficient in the martial arts many of my psychological insecurities started to subside. I was becoming more communicative and assertive, and I had a better self-image. My attitude toward others began to change. A few months after I started training, this new personality began to show: I was chosen Airman of the Month.

I also found that I was a member of a very elite brotherhood whose members were extremely loyal to each other. One night a Korean Air Policeman who worked as an interpreter on the base was going home through an alley that, like most alleys in Korea, was so narrow that people had to turn sideways to pass each other. Suddenly he was jumped by six slicky boys, young Korean muggers. One of the attackers had a knife. The Air Policeman raised his hand to ward off the blow, and the others jumped him. He was beaten up and robbed. It happened that the Air Policeman was a black belt in tang soo do. When the slicky boys found this out, they printed an apology in the local paper. It didn't do them any good. When you mess with one black belt, you take on the whole organization. One of our members tracked the attackers down. He killed one and injured two. The police prosecuted him, and he was sentenced to three years in prison. But he was out in two weeks.

After almost a year of daily practice, Mr. Shin told me I was ready for my black-belt test. Now every move I made would be observed by critical eyes. Mr. Shin and the other black belts mercilessly drilled me over and over on the various *heians* on which I might be tested and that I had already practiced to exhaustion hundreds of times. Every other technique I had learned was sharpened by constant criticism: "Press your hips forward . . . lift your knee higher . . . speed up . . . more spirit . . . do it again . . . bring the fist back with a snap . . . turn the toe in . . . keep the heel straight . . . don't hold your breath . . . breathe with the blow . . . relax . . . only tense when you need to . . . relax . . . don't be so tense."

I was a nervous and physical wreck by the time I was

scheduled to face the Board of Examiners in Seoul. My sergeant let me borrow a truck from the car pool for the forty-mile drive. It was the dead of winter. The roads were icy, and the drive took two hours. I arrived stiff with cold at the dojo (training hall) where the test was to be held.

The dojo was a big unheated building; wind was blowing through open spaces in the walls, designed to be windows. It was − 8° inside as well as out. I changed into my *gi* (karate uniform) and joined the other students kneeling along one side of the building. I was the only one from my school among two hundred strangers, other *kareteka* (karate practitioners) there to test for various ranks. The Board of Examiners, including Mr. Hwang Kee, the president of the Moo Duk Kwan Tang Soo Do Association (our parent organization), were in front at a table that held a stack of examination cards.

I watched as the others did their forms and free-sparred with selected black belts. At first I compared myself to the other novices and watched with interest. Within half an hour, however, my mind could only focus on how cold and stiff I was from sitting on my knees, unable to move. After about three hours of sitting with body and mind numb, I heard my name called.

I went before the examiners, bowed, and heard someone tell me to do a *heian*. I couldn't remember the form I was to do, even though I had done it countless times. My concentration had been broken by the cold and my nervousness. I told the examiners the *heian* didn't come to mind. I was ordered back to my place. I had to wait four more hours, until the others finished testing, before I could leave.

I was miserable on the drive alone back to the base. Over and over again I did the form I had forgotten in my thoughts, then I decided to put the experience out of my mind. If I dwelled on it, I would be preparing to fail again. I had to prepare to succeed, and I had to begin planting those seeds now. Subconsciously I was beginning to evolve a philosophy of inner strength.

Mr. Shin said nothing about my failure. I trained for an additional three months before he suggested that I take the exam again. I had put the first exam out of my mind and only saw myself succeeding this time. I visualized myself doing the form perfectly, any form that was requested. And I saw myself completing the rest of the test successfully.

This time I was better prepared to deal with the physical and psychological hardships. The test was just as grueling as the previous one, but I was ready when my name was called. I did my forms and some one-step punching and board breaking, and then I free-sparred against a black belt. Everything went as I had visualized. When I returned to the base I felt better about myself. I had done the best I could.

A few weeks later, Mr. Shin took me aside after class. Smiling, he told me I had passed the exam. He bowed formally and presented me with a new black belt with my name written on it in Korean and a silver pin for my lapel. That pin was soon to take on a special significance for me.

One night a few weeks later, I was walking in the

village in civvies when five slicky boys started to attack me. I was preparing to confront them when they saw the pin on my lapel. They scattered. I felt like Clark Kent wearing his Superman costume.

Earning my black belt changed my life; for the first time in my life, I had accomplished something difficult on my own. I had belief in myself and the strength to accomplish more. Every success gives you the strength to go on to further success. I also found that working toward a goal was even more rewarding than achieving it.

Being a *shodan* (first-degree black belt) was like getting a Bachelor of Arts degree. Belt ranks are like school levels, starting at elementary school (white belt) and proceeding (with different colors, depending on the martial-arts style) through elementary school, junior high school, high school, and finally college.

Earning my black belt meant I was ready for more advanced study; I was well aware that I was still a student. One thing I had learned is that there was always someone better. Even the masters had masters. But one of the best things about karate training was that I no longer worried about my ability to take care of myself. Usually a man fights because he wants to prove he is better or tougher than someone else; with nothing to prove, I had no need to fight.

By the end of my tour of duty I had been promoted to Airman First Class. Not only did I have a first-degree black belt in tang soo do; I had earned a third-degree brown belt in judo as well.

My tour in Korea was the first time I had ever been out of the United States. The poverty in Korea was an eye-opener for me. I had grown up poor, but I always had enough to eat. Some of the Koreans I saw had barely enough to eat from day to day. Life was a constant struggle for them, with no hope of improvement in their lives. I realized how lucky I was to be an American. Until then I had taken for granted all the opportunities and benefits America offers.

I was reassigned to the States, but so many other GIs were en route at the same time that I had to wait for space in Tokyo. I used the time to visit the Shotokan, home of Japanese karate, and to watch some judo at the Kodakan, the famous judo school. I came away impressed with the discipline of the training, which was more regimented than in Korea.

When I landed in San Francisco, I had to call Dianne at home to tell her that I would be arriving in Los Angeles within the hour. I had only nine cents in my pocket, and a dime was necessary to make any kind of call—even collect. With less than two minutes to spare before my plane left, I finally found someone who gave me a dime for nine cents.

I had a real homecoming. Dianne was at the airport with my mother, stepfather, and in-laws. She looked beautiful. But she had also changed; she was only seventeen when we were married, and in the fifteen months we had been apart, she had matured.

The Army had given me a thirty-day leave, and Dianne had saved eight hundred dollars from her job and my allotment checks—enough money for us to go to Las Vegas for a holiday alone. The trip turned out to be a disaster. On our first night in Vegas we decided to party it up and then go back to our hotel room and make passionate love. We both got so plastered that Dianne passed out on the floor of our room. I had just enough strength to carry her to the bed. Then the room started spinning. I woke up on the floor with Dianne asking me to go down to the pharmacy and get her some aspirin. Reluctantly, I did. We spent the day trying to get over our hangovers. I don't think either of us had ever felt so sick.

We had grown apart, and resuming life together was stressful. We'd been married young, and each of us had matured and changed. It took a while for us to get to know each other again, but we were determined to get through this readjustment period. We rented a small apartment on the outskirts of March Air Force Base in Riverside, where I was an E4, or buck sergeant, in the Military Police.

Meanwhile, I kept practicing tang soo do by myself. There was a large tree in front of our house, and whenever I had the time I would pound on it with my fists to keep my knuckles hard and calloused. My neighbor swore that he could feel the vibrations in his house.

There were no karate classes at the base, but there was a judo club that I immediately joined. I soon started competing in matches as a brown belt and was sent to Seattle, Washington, for the 15th Air Force Judo Championships.

In judo, competitors are matched by weight, not by rank. There were about forty of us in my weight division; we ranged from white belts (beginners) to black belts, all competing together. I wound up beating three black belts and made it into the semifinals along with two black belts and a white belt.

Before my match I hoped I would be lucky enough to draw the white belt as my opponent. I was confident I could beat him and then make it to the finals. We drew numbers from a basket to determine the match-ups, and I got my wish—I drew the white belt.

I took it for granted that I had it made. In my mind I had already won the match. After all, I had beaten three black belts. But I had forgotten that my opponent had gotten to the top the same way. This overconfidence was a big mistake on my part.

When we got on the mat I expected an easy win, but all of a sudden I was fighting for my life. I wasn't mentally prepared, as I had been in the day's previous matches, and I wound up losing to my adversary, who was extremely strong. After the match I congratulated my opponent and told him he was one of the strongest men I had ever encountered. "I'm a lumberjack by trade," he explained. I thought to myself that I had been lucky; he probably could have torn my limbs off as easily as he did tree limbs.

Meanwhile, I kept practicing tang soo do by myself at the base wherever I could find space. One day some GIs saw me doing some kicks. They were intrigued and asked me to teach them what I knew. Naturally I was delighted at the chance, so I went through channels and got the authority to start a karate club on the base, using the basketball court as a training area.

On the opening night of the karate club I had to put on a demonstration and give a little talk. I was twenty-one years old, and the thought of speaking before an audience still petrified me. I decided that there was only one thing to do: write out a speech and memorize it. I wrote down what I wanted to say and then tape-recorded myself reading it. I listened to the tape for hours, repeating the speech over and over. Finally I had it down pat.

There were a few hundred people in the auditorium that night—soldiers, officers, and their families. I could feel myself sweating from the tension of having to speak. I was so scared I didn't see or hear anyone. Then I remembered that I had failed my first black-belt test because of nerves, and how determined I had been that it would never happen again. I walked up to the microphone and said, "Good evening, ladies and gentlemen, my name is Chuck Norris . . ."

I don't remember anything else. To this day I have no idea what I said. I put the microphone down, and as I was doing my demonstration, I kept asking myself, "Did I say anything?"

Afterward I asked Dianne what she had thought of my talk. "Oh," she said, "it was just fine." Of course, she would have said that anyway. I doubt that I could ever have addressed those people without the confidence I had gotten from my martial-arts training.

47

That speech helped crack the egg of insecurity I had carried around for twenty-one years. I had broken another barrier in my life and achieved another success because I had done something that I had always been too afraid to do before. I had faced fear and conquered it, another stage of inner strength.

The karate club at the base became a big success. My students got into such excellent physical shape that they scored highest of all the soldiers on the base in the physical-fitness tests. The more successful we became, the more cooperation we received. Lieutenant General Archie J. Old, the 15th Air Force Commander, even joined our club and became an honorary black belt.

I was sent to a combat school for ten weeks of additional training, along with sixty other GIs from all over the country. Most of us were from either the Military Police or Intelligence. Every day we had four hours of classroom work and four hours of physical training in karate, judo, knife fighting, and jujitsu. I wound up becoming the karate instructor and, at the end of the course, won the Outstanding Student Award.

After my discharge in August 1962, I decided to visit my grandmother in Oklahoma. Dianne, who was then seven months pregnant, was afraid to make the trip. She'd had a miscarriage soon after we were married, and now that she was pregnant again she was determined to take it easy so she would not jeopardize the baby.

My brother Wieland and I drove to Wilson in my '55 Chevy. One afternoon, when I was in town, I ran into my father standing in front of a bar. For years I had wondered what we would say to each other if we ever met again. In a sense I feared such a meeting. But as so often happens when you have an anticipated confrontation, none of my fears became a reality. We exchanged only a few perfunctory words. I told him that I was married and that my wife was expecting a baby. "Great," he said. And that was about it.

I was saddened by the change in him. He looked old and seemed tired. Drink had taken its toll on him. I realized that we were really strangers. We had shared so few good times together that, although I loved him because he was my father, I really had no reason to like him. That was the last time I saw him.

I don't hold any grudges against him, though. He was what he was. You can't condemn people because of what they are. I knew that when he couldn't deal with certain things, such as family responsibilities or financial problems, he'd hit the bottle. That was just something he couldn't control. It was a shame because he missed so much.

Wieland and I had an adventure on the way home that confirmed my belief in America. We left Wilson on a Sunday and had driven only a few miles when a wheel bearing went out. I pulled into a gas station. The attendant said that all the garages in town were closed, but there was a fellow up the street who worked on cars. I drove to the man's home and asked whether he could fix my car. "Sure," he said, "I can do it. Take my car and have lunch in town. I'll have you ready to roll by the time you get back."

He didn't know us, and yet he was lending us a brand-new car. When we returned from lunch the wheel bearing was installed and cost only ten dollars, half the price I would have paid elsewhere.

Sometimes I forget that there are places in America where people are warm, generous, and honest and believe that others are also honest.

My stepfather arranged an interview for me with a supervisor at Northrop Aircraft, the defense contractor where he was employed. In September 1962 I was hired as a file clerk in records management for a salary of $320 a month. Our son Mike was born two months later. Since we had no money, he was delivered at UCLA, where patients were charged according to what they could afford.

My boss at Northrop was a woman named Agnes Dean, who was very supportive of me. She knew that my real goal was to be in the police department, but there was a year's waiting list just to take the next test. Since I had only a high school diploma and needed some college courses to qualify, I had to study long hours, poring over correspondence-course books. Agnes frequently allowed me to take time off to meet with various police departments.

The other workers at Northrop were also so nice that

one day I became inspired to write a poem about them. It was my first literary attempt. To my surprise, Agnes thought so much of it that she had it circulated throughout the company.

Although the desk job I had was not to my liking, I had to earn a living, and at least I was bringing home a weekly paycheck. As I think back on those years now I realize that very often in life one has to do what is necessary at the time. Later the detour may turn out to have been fortuitous.

Had I gone directly to work in a police department without working at Northrop first, chances are I would be a policeman today. My life would have been totally different. I would not have become a karate champion, which led me into acting.

To supplement my income from Northrop I began teaching karate in my parents' back yard after work. Since it was impossible to buy a *gi* (karate uniform) in the States at that time, Dianne made a pattern from my Korean *gi* and copied it for me.

My first students were my brothers. Aaron was now nine, and Wieland was eighteen. I had started teaching them months before, when I had come back from Korea on leave. Another of my students was my cousin Ronnie, who was four years older than I. When we were growing up, he used to push me around and hold me down, and there had never been anything I could do about it. Now I was his karate instructor.

After a class one night, he said to me, "Let's wrestle." I tried to decline, but he was insistent. Ronnie was quite

51

strong, but I had been practicing judo for three years; we tussled for a few minutes and I set him up for a judo throw. In judo practice I usually held on to my partner and guided him to the ground. But I threw Ronnie about eight feet into the air. I was a little ashamed of myself later, but it sure did feel good at the time.

After several months, word began to spread around the neighborhood about the Norris brothers. We started getting invitations from the Rotary Club and other organizations to put on demonstrations. The demos were exciting because they gave me a chance to demonstrate my skill in a sport that was still new in the States. Besides, it was fun working with my brothers.

Aaron was a cute little fellow, so we had a bit in which he would throw us "big guys" around. Audiences loved it, and so did Aaron—for the first five or six demonstrations. But after a while he decided he'd had enough. One night a club called and asked us to put on a demonstration. Wieland was agreeable, but Aaron said he didn't want to do it anymore. I insisted. He cried all the way to the club, but after we started our routine and he got into it, everything was fine.

The demos helped me realize that people were interested in karate. I felt that the time was right and that I could risk opening a school in Torrance, where we lived. My stepfather cosigned a loan for six hundred dollars—enough for the first month's rent, mats for the floor, two big mirrors for the walls, and paint. I opened my studio in a 15' x 30' storefront on the corner of two main streets. The entire family pitched in to paint it, and soon the store was transformed into a studio. We even hand-lettered a sign saying "Chuck Norris Karate" and hung it outside. My "office" was a tiny desk in a corner.

Actually, we were something of a traffic hazard. Cars passing by used to slow down to look through the windows at the classes taking place. This was great, because some of the passers-by became interested in what we were doing and signed up. I started with ten students who paid ten dollars apiece per month, which entitled them to classes plus a chance to work out every night for as many hours as they wanted.

For the next two years I continued to work at Northrop from 8:00 A.M. to 5:00 P.M. weekdays. I'd drive home, where Dianne would have dinner ready for me. I would gulp it down and then race to the dojo and teach from 6:00 P.M. to 10:00 P.M. It was a strenuous period, but I knew that if I was going to succeed at anything I would have to strive extra hard.

When I was teaching I had to change my *gi* two times a night because I perspired so much from the effort. The only time I had free to spend with my family was on Saturday evenings and Sundays. It wasn't much, but I felt that the quality of the time I spent with them was more important than the quantity. I was lucky that Dianne was supportive, for we had a new dream—a dream that I would have enough students to be able to quit my job at Northrop.

I had learned over the years that when I want something I must first establish the goal in my mind and form a mental picture of it. I try to imagine all the obstacles that will get in my way. I mentally prepare to overcome them. I visualize the goal as being already accomplished. Then I muster all my determination and persistence so that I can stick with the project long enough to succeed.

As far as I'm concerned, ability is not the major prerequisite in achieving any goal—determination and persistence will overcome any obstacle. I believe there are few things that can't be accomplished if you train and mentally prepare yourself properly. In addition, you must always keep a mental image of your goal. This was another aspect of my personal philosophy, which I was coming to think of as a way to inner strength.

After teaching in the dojo for two years, I finally had thirty students, an additional three hundred dollars per month gross on top of my income from Northrop. My goal was to have forty students. The time came for me to take my exam for the police department, but I let it pass because the more I taught, the more I realized that I wanted to be a full-time karate instructor.

Teaching wasn't easy, but seeing the results of my efforts continually motivated me. I had discovered a gratification in teaching that I had never experienced before. It's a wonderful feeling to see a young boy walk into class for the first time, so shy that he can't look into another boy's eyes or even relate to or communicate with other kids his age. Within weeks of his first karate lesson, his character and attitude change. He begins to look the other kids in the eye, and he even says hi. Soon this youngster who couldn't perform a basic kick without stumbling gets to the point where he can execute techniques with blinding speed, as graceful and elegant as a bird in flight.

In 1964 I quit Northrop—a frightening step—and opened a second school in Redondo Beach with forty students at fifteen dollars per month. But I needed even more students to pick up the slack from my old Northrop job. I realized that in order to recruit more students I needed to get some exposure. If I were to win a tournament, I might get a write-up in a karate magazine or in my local paper. That would help me get more students. I considered this new goal—winning a tournament to get publicity and more students—to be within the realm of my ability. I decided to go all out for it.

A combination of discipline and learning leads to confidence. Remember that everyone is a beginner at some point in his life; even your teacher was once a pupil.

Face your fears and conquer them. If you do something you have previously been afraid to do, you will begin to crack the egg of your insecurity. Accomplishing something difficult gives you the strength to go on to further success.

With nothing to prove, there is no need for a confrontation. When you get to the point where you have to fight, you've already lost the battle.

THREE

I WAS TWENTY-FOUR years old when, in 1964, I entered my first karate tournament. I was older than most of the competitors in this new sport, but I was determined to give it a try. The tournament was held in Salt Lake City, Utah, and I drove there from Los Angeles with three of my students. The trip took sixteen hours in an old Ford Falcon, and we almost didn't make it because of a snowstorm en route.

We arrived a few hours before the tournament was to begin. I had dieted all week so I could qualify for the lightweight division (below 155 pounds). When I got onto the scale I was shocked to discover that I was five pounds over the weight limit, which put me in the black-belt middleweight class. I was famished from the long drive and from having starved myself, so I went out for breakfast and really laid into the pancakes, eggs, and bacon. When I returned to the stadium I had to weigh in again. This time I was only a pound and a half over the limit; the scale I had been on earlier was off. Without the big breakfast I could have been in with the lightweights; now I would be one of the lightest middleweights. I went into the locker room with my students, and we changed into our uniforms.

I warmed up with my students, who were in the beginner and intermediate divisions, and when my name was called I went into the ring.

The fighting area was the size of a boxing ring. The matches were officiated by a center referee who was assisted by four side judges, one at each corner of the ring. Each judge had a red flag in one hand and a white flag in the other; each contestant wore either a white or a red tag in his belt.

A point was given for an *ippon* (a full point or killing blow)—a single focused attack, undeflected or unblocked, that landed directly on one of the vital areas of the body. It had to be delivered with good form and balance, proper distance, and explosive but controlled force. A karate fighter was supposed to be able to kick and punch yet stop a blow a fraction of an inch from its target, the notion being that if you can hit, you can miss.

When a point was scored, the judges held up a red or white flag to indicate which fighter had earned it. Three of the five judges had to have seen a scoring blow for it to be awarded. All of this was new and confusing to me because

1 had never fought under such formal conditions before, and I had little time to take everything in.

My first match was with someone I knew, a fighter from Colorado who had also been in Korea. We bowed before entering the ring and then took up our starting positions in the center. On the command *"Hajime"* ("Begin!"), given by the center judge, we started. Each of us tried to penetrate the other's defenses. I recall little about that first fight or the one that followed, other than the fact that I won. There was no time for elation, however. My third fight was with a well-known Hawaiian fighter. My best weapon, actually my only one, was my kicks. He beat me with a punch.

When the smoke from the heavy competition cleared, my three students had won and I had lost.

While I drove all the way back to Los Angeles, my students clung to their trophies and I thought about why I had lost. Philosophies are created from experiences in life. I realized that although I might lose another tournament, I would never be defeated in the same way. I understood that the only time you really lose is when you don't learn from the experience. Life is a series of experiences, and if you gain a lesson from them, whether they are good or bad, you really don't lose. I said to myself, I'll never lose that way again—never. And I never did.

I went back to the studio to practice, more determined than ever to find out what I was doing wrong. I was so upset with myself that on the first night of training I worked out so hard I lost six pounds! My students dropped an average of four to five pounds that night too, thanks to the workout I put us all through.

The next scheduled tournament was the Internationals in Long Beach, California. It was the largest karate tournament in the world, with more than three thousand fighters entered. I decided to stay in the middleweight division. But once again I lost. Instead of feeling dejected, I began training again with increased vigor and concentrating on my weak points: I had to improve my timing; I had to learn to close the space between my opponent and me more quickly; and I had to develop more confidence as a fighter. I also worked on perfecting some of the techniques I had learned in Korea, including the spinning back kick. I felt I could use it effectively in future contests because it was still unfamiliar to many Americans.

In May 1964, Dianne gave birth to our second son. She had seen a commercial on television for Erik cigarettes, featuring a handsome Scandinavian. "I like that name," she told me. "If we have a son, let's name him Eric." I didn't like the model but I, too, liked the name.

Soon after Eric was born, I entered Tak Kubota's All-Stars Tournament in Los Angeles. In those days the point system for scoring varied from tournament to tournament and from region to region. In some matches the winner was the first contestant to score two points; in others, it was the contestant who had scored the most points when the time was up. In the All-Stars Tournament a match lasted two minutes; the fighter with the most points at the end of that time was the winner. The Japanese judges, all senior black belts themselves, were stingy with points. Unless a technique was flawless, they usually awarded only a half point.

I made it to the finals. The man I had to fight for the championship was Ron Marchini, a Japanese stylist and a strong, consistent fighter who incorporated judo into his repertoire. Neither of us was able to score on the other until about halfway into the match, when Ron feinted a kick but unexpectedly followed through with a stepping punch, putting his knuckleprints on my solar plexus. His timing and control were superb. Three of the side judges held out their white flags horizontally to signal a half point for Ron. The other judge crossed his flags in front of his face, indicating that he had not seen the blow. The match was restarted. Ron decided to fight defensively. Each time I attacked with my kicks, he moved out of the ring, using up precious time. We clashed in the center of the ring, both of us landing blows. The match was halted momentarily as the judges decided that neither of us had scored. As we returned to the center of the ring, I glanced at the clock. There were just fifteen seconds remaining. The second after we bowed to commence the match, I grabbed Ron's *gi*, swept his feet out from under him, and punched him in the ribs. I followed up with a *shuto* (edge of the hand) chop to the neck just as the buzzer went off, signaling the end of the fight. Four judges held their red flags up vertically to indicate that I had scored an *ippon* (full point).

It was my first win and a high point of my life. The satisfaction of knowing that I had finally won a tournament increased my confidence and gave me the impetus and positive frame of mind I needed to continue in competition.

I decided to try for the California state title. I went to the tournament with twelve of my students, ranging from white to black belts. I won the Middleweight Championship by the expeditious use of the spinning back kick, which was to become my trademark. But I lost the Grand Championship to Tony Tulleners.

Eleven of my twelve students won their matches, and the Norris School dominated the tournament! Since the match-ups for the first fight are often determined by who is standing next to you, it got to the point that when other competitors saw our school patch on a *gi*, they would try to avoid lining up with that student so they would not have to fight him.

One morning soon after the tournament I left my house to teach my first karate class of the day. I started to get into my car and noticed that the windows were blackened inside. An electrical short had caused a fire in the engine and the dashboard. I hitchhiked to school, and my brother-in-law lent me his '39 Chevy to drive until I could afford to buy another car.

Unfortunately the old clunker didn't have turn signals. I

made a right-hand turn without signaling, and a policeman stopped me. He looked at my driver's license and the old car. "I don't normally write citations for this kind of violation," he said, "but today I am going to." Great, I thought, I don't have a dime to my name, and he writes me a ticket.

Not long ago I was driving my new Mercedes, doing about ten miles per hour over the speed limit. An officer pulled me over and looked at the car and my license. "Slow it down, Chuck," he said, and he went back to his patrol car. When I could afford a ticket, I didn't get one.

In 1965 I entered and won several tournaments, including the Winter Nationals in San Jose, California. I became a major championship competitor by again defeating Ron Marchini for the Grand Champion title. This win encouraged me to set my sights on the Internationals, the most prestigious of all the tournaments. It was held in August 1966.

I won the middleweight division of the Internationals by beating a fighter who had beaten me the year before. That win felt great. But the feeling didn't last long; my fight for the Grand Championship was with Allen Steen, a big fellow from Dallas, Texas, who used his height to his advantage and who had long legs with tremendous power. He had just defeated Joe Lewis, one of the best of the new fighters, and I thought, Anyone who can beat Joe must be good. I was right. I lost to Allen, too. That was my last tournament of 1966. I took the rest of the year off to prepare for 1967.

I realized that although I had gotten good results with the spinning back kick in my first few tournaments, my opponents were now anticipating it. To be able to compete effectively in future matches, I would have to increase my repertoire. At that time most karate fighters were either good kickers or good with their hands, but few of them could blend kicks and punches together.

Many of my friends were top karate instructors. Normally it is difficult to go from dojo to dojo to train because each style is different, but some of my friends allowed me to work out with them.

Fumio Demura, an expert in shito ryu, showed me how to blend my hands and feet together and gave me a good arsenal of kicks and punches. I learned hand and foot combinations from Hidetaka Nishiyama, a master of shotokan karate.

Tutamu Oshima encouraged me to go beyond my physical limitations. He pushed me to the point where I didn't think I could do any more, and then he encouraged me to go even further. He taught me to go beyond the pain barrier, thus further developing the inner strength that lies within all of us. I went to Oshima's training camp in Big Bear, California, where he kept his students in a *kibadashi* (a karate stance in which feet are extended twice as far apart as the width of the shoulders) for an hour and a half at a time without moving. Then he would get us into a cat stance (a position in which most of the body weight is placed on the rear foot and only the ball of the extended foot touches the ground) for forty-five minutes on each leg. It was physical discipline and mental torture, but I proved to myself that I could go the distance.

Jun Chung (who taught hapkido) helped me perfect some of my Korean techniques. He also taught me some aikido as well as body pressure points for close-in encounters. Al Thomas (a jujitsu instructor) worked with me on choke techniques. Ed Parker, the father of American kenpo karate and promoter of the Internationals, spent hours in his dojo teaching me his system. Gene LeBell, an expert in wrestling, boxing, judo, and karate, helped me put together everything I had learned. Gene is one of the toughest men I have ever met as well as one of the most versatile people in the martial arts.

All of these men were generous with their time and talent. It says a great deal for the martial-arts community that, although we are competitive, we are all willing to share our knowledge.

I took something from each style and modified it for myself, incorporating it into what I already knew. Soon I had such a variety of techniques that I knew an opponent would find it almost impossible to ever pinpoint a specific movement and zero in on it.

In 1967 I entered the All-American Karate Championship, which was being held at the Madison Square Garden in New York. Hundreds of karate fighters from all over the world were to compete in an elimination tournament.

I arrived in New York the day before the tournament and went to bed early. I knew from experience that it was important to have a good night's sleep so that I would be totally relaxed on the day of the fight. When I got into bed, my mind was racing, but I forced myself to imagine that I was in a completely dark room. I concentrated on that total darkness until I slipped off to sleep. Another trick I sometimes use is to imagine that I am watching a movie screen that suddenly goes black.

I awoke on the morning of the tournament completely refreshed. Long before nutritionists began suggesting that athletes observe high-carbohydrate diets before competing, I knew what I should have the day of a fight. My body told me what was right to eat, and on this morning I had a piece of fruit, some pancakes, and a cup of tea.

When I arrived at the Garden, I saw all the other competitors standing around, talking to old friends, or joking and laughing. Some, burning with nervous energy, paced the sidewalk. Friends came over to me and we shook hands and wished each other luck. There is a strong camaraderie among fighters. Many of the competitors had trained with me at my school, and I had sometimes worked out at theirs. There was never rivalry until we got in the ring, just strong friendly competitiveness. I felt a close bond with the others because I knew we shared the same thoughts and feelings. We were all warriors about to do battle.

I registered, paid my fee to enter the competition, and then went to the locker room. I took my freshly laundered uniform from my overnight bag and undressed, putting my clothes in a locker. My *gi* felt good, almost as though it were a part of my body. It had become my favorite clothing—loose in the shoulders, with sleeves and pants that snapped like a whip when I kicked or punched.

I tried to keep myself relaxed and in a calm state because I knew that when I was tense, I was burning energy. I wanted to be totally relaxed prior to fighting, conserving the energy that I would need when I stepped into the ring.

The tournament director called the black belts to line up for pairing. I went to the middle of the floor and let the line form on each side of me. Some of the black belts hung back to scout the opposition. They were trying to pick their opponents so they wouldn't have to exert themselves too much in their first match.

The various competitors, lightweights, middleweights, and heavyweights, were to fight in several different rings. The winners of all the matches would then face each other in a round robin until one man was left in each division. The Grand Champion would be the winner of the last match. I was competing in the middleweight black-belt division.

I settled down on the sidelines to watch the lower-ranked belts (below the rank of black) compete. Now that I had become tournament-wise, it was a matter of routine for me to study the other competitors, because I knew I might have to confront some of them later on. I watched the way fighters walked for signs of injury. I noticed the way they stretched and warmed up: a kicker warms up with kicks and combinations of kicks, usually working on the one he will use most when under pressure. A fighter with good hand techniques warms up with repetitions and the combinations he favors.

I studied the winners as well as the losers. The winners were the ones I would probably have to fight. The losers were men I might have to fight in the future. The techniques fighters scored with were my immediate concern. I visualized myself in the ring with whichever man I was watching. I inventoried my own techniques and matched them to his defense. I visualized myself taking his strengths from him while maintaining my own; if, for example, I could see myself blocking an opponent's powerful side kick and then scoring with my own technique, I would be able to do it when the real match began.

When I am competing, I take the matches one at a time. I concentrate my full energy on each match and not on the end result. My first goal is to beat my first opponent. On this day in 1967, I had my techniques wired and was in peak physical and mental condition. I had trained hard, and my reflexes were razor-sharp. I knew what I was going to do against each opponent because I had already visualized every match, so I wasn't under any pressure. I won my first eleven fights.

As one of the top contenders, I knew that my next fight would probably be with Hiroshi Nakamura, the All-Japan

Middleweight champion. I sat on the sidelines watching as Mr. Nakamura eliminated his opponent. A small, powerfully built man, Mr. Nakamura had moves that were smooth and polished but all of a pattern. His specialty was a front kick produced with blinding speed, followed by a straight punch delivered as easily and quickly as a snap of the fingers, only with enormous power.

I studied him carefully, just as, when I was in the ring, he sat at ringside scrutinizing me. But I had an edge on him: I had studied the Japanese styles of karate as well as the Korean. I knew what he knew, but he didn't know what I knew.

Mr. Nakamura wound up winning his ring, and I won mine, which meant that after dinner that night we would face each other for the Middleweight Championship.

Before dinner we went into the washroom. I approached him and said, "Good luck tonight, Mr. Nakamura."

"I think you are going to beat me," he said.

"No, you've got a good chance," I said. "I've been watching you, and you are very good."

Regardless of what I had told him, I knew I could beat him because I had already visualized the bout in my mind and was prepared for his attacks. I was also ready for his defenses, and I knew I would score my points. Despite this mental exercise of visualization and psyching-up before a bout, there were times when I didn't win. But I always felt that I was going to.

That night I went to dinner with Bob Wall, a karate champion and very close friend who had accompanied me from Los Angeles. We had a light meal at an inexpensive restaurant near our hotel and talked about the matches we had observed, the up-and-comers who would undoubtedly be heard from in the future. And we discussed the men I had fought and the strategies I might use against them in the future.

Normally I don't mind talking to anyone before a contest. No matter what I'm doing—having dinner, getting dressed, or wrapping my hands—I'm happy to have a conversation. But this carefree attitude changes once I step on the mat. Then, and only then, my concentration is totally on the task at hand: winning. I am not by nature an aggressive person. But I'm aggressive in life and on the mat when I have to be.

For example, when I sparred with black belts in my school I frequently lost. They could not understand why they could beat me in class but not in competition. In class, I had nothing to gain by winning. There was no challenge.

During a competition, however, I may smile and shake hands with people in the audience as I walk down the aisle toward the ring and my opponent, but when I get into the ring my whole attitude and personality change.

There are three facets to being a winner—mental, psychological, and physical. I prepare myself mentally by knowing my competitor's strengths and weaknesses and how I can take advantage of both; when I am mentally sharp I am aware of and see everything that goes on around me. I prepare psychologically by believing in my ability and knowing that I can win. I prepare physically by being in the best possible shape, able to execute my techniques to the best of my ability. When I'm at the top of my form I often hit an opponent even before my brain records it—I see an opening and go for it. I know that if I get physically tired I may lose the will to win.

There's an old adage I have always believed in: "He who fails to prepare prepares to fail." A winner thinks of winning while a loser thinks of losing. A winner says to himself, When I win . . . , whereas a loser says to himself, If I win. . . . A winner must have a positive attitude. He visualizes himself scoring the winning points, and he sees the referee raising his hand in victory. These positive images create the will and the impetus to succeed. But positive imaging is worthless unless you are psychologically, physically, and mentally prepared to win.

It's odd how many commonly held ideas are all wrong— the notion that you need a lot of raw courage to fight, for example. Courage isn't a prerequisite for winning; skill is something else again. One often sees fighters who believe that courage is all they need; they go in over their heads too early. They depend on courage rather than skill, and they often get hurt or lose. Sometimes an opponent runs into a punch or blocks improperly, resulting in an injury. Since karate is a competitive sport, there is always a chance of being hurt. But there has rarely been a death in karate competition, primarily because of the strict discipline involved.

71

It is a peculiarity of the real competitor that he is indifferent to being hurt. The mental concentration required to compete transcends consideration of physical pain. I don't concern myself about an injury unless it keeps me out of a match; sometimes I even do better when I am hurting because it gives me a heightened sense of awareness. Once I'm in the ring I forget about the pain. I believe that by bypassing it I can reach an even higher plane of awareness, thus pushing myself beyond my normal capabilities.

Bob and I returned to the Garden after dinner. I went into the locker room and took a fresh *gi* from the small bag Dianne had packed for me. There was a note tucked inside, with the message: "To my Champion. Bring home the trophy." It was signed "D." Dianne regularly hid a note in my *gi* when she couldn't be with me; it was always a pleasure to find it.

After putting on the *gi* I taped my big toes to the ones next to them with adhesive. Then I wrapped my hands with an Ace bandage to prevent any fingers from breaking. In the sixties, when semicontact karate was in its heyday, we didn't wear safety equipment, gloves, or padding on the feet, as is done today.

The rules in this tournament called for each match to be two minutes long. Whoever had scored the most points when the time expired was the winner.

When my name and Mr. Nakamura's were called out over the loudspeaker, I went to the ring. I was aware of the audience, but I didn't really hear it; the sound the spectators were making reminded me of a waterfall in the distance—roaring, continuous, and fierce. My heart started beating faster, pumping blood through my body and brain, giving me an adrenaline rush. I tried to pull all that energy up so I could use it to the maximum.

When I got into the ring I forced myself to relax by slowing down my breathing. It's very hard to move if you're tense; relaxed muscles collaborate with rather than contradict each other, and I knew I could move faster when relaxed than when tense.

Then I turned my attention to the four judges and the referee. Three out of the five must see a scoring blow or kick for a point to be awarded. It was imperative that I be in a position for two of the corner judges and the referee to see my techniques. The referee rarely changed sides, so I moved to a spot where he and two of the corner judges could have a clear view of my right leg, my most formidable weapon.

I had already visualized the entire fight in my mind. My strategy was to take away Mr. Nakamura's strong techniques. From my observation of his bouts I was certain that his first move was going to be his front kick. And I was right. He came right at me with it. But it was fast, faster than I had estimated. As soon as I saw him start to move I shifted aside, blocked his front kick, and hit him in the stomach. I scored one point.

I anticipated that his next attack would be a front kick followed by a punch. Again, I was right. He snapped the kick, and I shifted to the right, away from it. As he threw the punch, I blocked and countered with my own punch, which scored.

In those days, when Japanese stylists threw a kick they never faked or feinted—the kick went straight to the target. They were not accustomed to someone faking a kick to one area and landing it elsewhere. Knowing this, I faked a kick to the stomach. As Mr. Nakamura started to block, I continued the kick to his head. Another point for me. I scored regularly enough to wind up beating him 12 to 1 for the Middleweight Championship.

After that bout I fought the Lightweight Champion and won. Next I was scheduled to fight the Heavyweight Champion, Joe Lewis, for the Grand Championship. Joe had an awesome reputation. A natural athlete, he was also a weight lifter and had earned his black belt in 1964, after only seven months of lessons during his stint with the Marine Corps in Okinawa. In 1966, with only twenty-two months of training, he had entered his first tournament— the National Karate Championship—and won it.

When Joe moved from North Carolina to Los Angeles he came to my school to practice. When we first sparred together I could score on him quite easily. After a couple of months of our training together, however, I found it extremely difficult to score any points on him because he was familiar with my style. We had fought each other in the Tournament of Champions only three months earlier, and I had won by a decision.

Joe had all the qualities he needed to be a world champion: size, speed, and strength. He was a formidable opponent, and I knew if I compared myself to him I would be very discouraged. Making comparisons was a negative thing to do, and I didn't intend to put myself in a negative frame of mind.

Joe was a very smart fighter whose two principal weapons were a lightning-fast side kick and a quick and powerful back fist. He was also physically and mentally intimidating. He instinctively understood what the Japanese refer to as kyo (weakness). He managed to control his opponents by attacking their greatest weaknesses, whether of mind, body, or spirit. If I let myself be intimidated by him I would lose, because I would be thinking about losing rather than winning. I believe that if you consider the possibility that you will lose, you will, because your subconscious mind will accept it as a fact.

In order to beat Joe I would have to be aggressive from the start, forcing him to think defensively rather than offensively. I was in top physical shape, so I knew I wouldn't get tired. I had my techniques down pat, and my reflexes were sharp. I was also psychologically determined to win.

The moment the referee told us to begin, Joe nailed me with a side kick in the ribs. One point for him. I realized that he was trying to put me on the defensive. I knew that if I allowed that to happen he would run right over me, so I became the aggressor. I didn't give him time to think about anything except defending against my constant attacks. Of course, I used up more energy than he did, but because I was in such good condition I could keep it up without tiring. I finally scored on him with a reverse punch (a punch delivered by the hand opposite the forward leg). Just as time was running out, I scored again with a back fist to the face. I won the Grand Championship by one point.

Since 8:00 A.M. that morning, I'd had thirteen fights in eleven hours. I wanted nothing more than a good night's sleep. But as I was leaving the stadium Bruce Lee came over to congratulate me. I knew of him, but we had never met. I had seen him put on a terrific demonstration at the Internationals a couple of years earlier, and I was familiar with his work as an actor on the *Green Hornet* television series.

After discovering that we were staying at the same hotel, we walked back together and talked about the martial arts and our philosophies. We were deeply involved in conversation as we went up together on the elevator. We stopped on his floor, and I stepped out with him.

It was then 11:45 P.M., but our conversation led us to exchange techniques right there in the hallway. The next time I looked at my watch, it was 7:00 A.M.! We had worked out together for seven hours! Bruce was so dynamic that it had seemed like only twenty minutes to me. It was the first time Bruce and I met and worked out together, but it was not to be the last.

You can always do a little more than you thought you could if you push yourself beyond what you think are your limitations.

There are three facets to being a winner: mental, psychological, and physical. Remember that he who fails to prepare in each area prepares to fail. A loser says to himself, If I win . . . A winner says to himself, When I win. . . .

FOUR

BRUCE LEE AND I spent many hours working out together in the secluded back yard of his modest home in Culver City, California. He had all types of equipment there, including a *Mook Jung* (wood practice dummy with sticks for arms and feet), a *makiwara* (straw-padded striking post for practicing punches), padded chest protectors, and boxing equipment.

We trained once or twice a week for three or four hours at a time. Bruce was a very capable and knowledgeable martial artist. Pound for pound, he was one of the strongest men I have ever met.

In those days, probably because of the wing chun (Chinese boxing) training he had had in Hong Kong before coming to America, Bruce didn't believe in high kicks. He kicked only below the waist. I finally convinced him that it was important to be versatile enough to kick anywhere. He took my suggestion seriously and had the motivation to learn. Within six months he could kick with precision, power, and speed to any area of the body. In return, he taught me some of his kung-fu techniques, including linear or straight punches that I was able to use in my own repertoire.

After workouts, we frequently drove in his car to Chinatown for lunch. Driving with him was always an adventure. He kept a small *makiwara* board on his lap or on the seat next to him. Every time we were caught in traffic or came to a stoplight he would beat on the board with either his fist or his knuckles to keep his hands hard.

Bruce loved *dim sum* (a Chinese breakfast of assorted dishes) and was so expert with chopsticks that he could pick up a grain of rice, toss it in the air, and catch it again. During meals we discussed our parallel martial-arts philosophies. We both believed that in order to grow as martial artists we needed to expand our abilities in all areas. Even then Bruce was taking boxing lessons, incorporating the footwork and some of the punches into his style.

We became good friends, close enough for him to share his dream with me: he wanted to be a film star. Everything he did was a stepping-stone toward that. He worked as a stunt coordinator on films and had many private students in the film business, including James Coburn, Steve McQueen, and the Academy Award-winning writer Stirling Silliphant. His students were usually his biggest fans, and they were often responsible for getting him employment on films.

Bruce lived and breathed the martial arts. I still recall the night I dropped in on him at home and found him in the den watching television. He was lying on his back in front of the TV set with his young son, Brandon, sitting on his stomach. Bruce had leg weights wrapped around his ankles. He had barbells in his hands. While bouncing Brandon on his stomach, he was inhaling and exhaling, thus tightening the muscles of his abdomen. At the same time, he was doing leg-ups and arm exercises.

I was impressed by the fact that, somehow, Bruce managed to turn everything he did, even entertaining his son, into a strengthening exercise. I suspect that if his wife, Linda, had asked him to dry the dishes, Bruce would have juggled them in the air to improve his hand-eye coordination.

His biggest problem—and, I think, his greatest weakness—was the fact that he didn't know how to turn off his engine. He never learned how to relax, to step back and smell the roses. He was driven—maybe *obsessed* is a better word for it—to be the most famous martial artist in the world.

Meanwhile Dianne had started, with my encouragement, to study karate. She attended my regular class for her first two lessons. As we were driving home after the first session, she said, "You never paid any attention to me throughout the whole class. I could have done anything wrong and you would never have noticed." The next night

I spent extra time helping her. On the way home that night, she said, "You picked on me throughout the whole class." I knew this would be a problem I could never solve, so I asked my brother Aaron to teach her.

Some months later, Aaron enlisted in the Army. A week later Wieland enlisted too. They were both assigned to the same camp for basic training. Aaron later told me that he and Wieland would sneak out at midnight to meet in a field behind Aaron's compound. Such meetings were against regulations, but it was typical of them to violate the rules so they could spend time together. We had all grown up close, and I missed my little brothers.

Soon after they enlisted, I decided to go to New York to defend my All-American title. Dianne announced to me that she intended to enter the women's division. She told me of her dream: she visualized us in the ring, the All-American male and female champions, holding up our trophies in triumph.

"Honey," I said, "some of these women in the tournament have been training for years. There are some tough female black belts, especially in the New York area. You are only a blue belt [a grade above white belt, or beginner]. To win the competition you are going to have to fight all the different belt ranks."

But Dianne was determined that we would both win, and I was unable to talk her out of competing. I knew that what she had in mind was just a dream. At the same time, I thought it would be good experience for her to enter one tournament and see what it was like, to know what I had to go through. I wasn't concerned about Dianne winning or losing. My main concern was that she not get hurt.

I sat at ringside with some of Dianne's relatives, who had driven down from Rhode Island to see her compete. My heart was in my mouth when I saw my wife in the ring. I knew all too well the strain she was under. We cheered Dianne on until we were hoarse, and she won her first two matches. Was I proud! But her third match was against Stephanie Revander, a New Yorker who trained under George Cofield of the Tong Dojo in Brooklyn.

I had seen Stephanie in the ring. She was so aggressive that many men would have had a difficult time with her. In an earlier bout, she had punched one girl in the face. In another, she had ripped an opponent's *gi* off her back.

I found George, her instructor, at ringside and asked him to make certain that Stephanie didn't punch Dianne in the face. George reported back to me that Stephanie had agreed to my request. Dianne did well against Stephanie, but she was overpowered and lost. During the match she got punched hard in the arm. The blow caused a hematoma. This condition lasted for about two weeks, during which time her arm shook spasmodically.

Dianne's hope of having us both win trophies went out the window. She had a goal, but it wasn't a realistic one. Even though she had visualized it, she wasn't prepared physically to achieve it. She decided to retire, defeated. Since both of our young sons had also taken up karate, she felt that three *karateka* in the family was enough.

As predicted, Joe Lewis and I both made it into the

finals that night. Before the match I visualized Joe's best techniques. I knew I would have to be careful of his side kick, followed up by his back fist. If he missed with the back fist he would probably grab and punch me. I created the fight in my mind, planning my strategy according to the old maxim: something vividly imagined is often close to the actual experience.

Thanks to my mental-image drills I had a sense of confidence when my bout with Joe commenced. I didn't stand in the ring worrying about what he was going to do or what was going to happen. I had visualized almost every possibility, and I was prepared as well as determined to win.

Our title match was extremely close, because we knew each other's strong points and moved only when there was an opening. But my mental imaging had prepared me for every eventuality, and I defeated Joe by one point.

It was around this time that I began reading books such as Napoleon Hill's *Laws of Success* and Dr. Joseph Murphy's *The Power of Your Subconscious Mind*. I discovered that I had intuitively been doing what these authors suggested—using visualization and my subconscious mind to help me achieve my goals. The books and lectures enhanced my own thinking.

My next fight was in Cleveland, Ohio, at the National Tournament of Champions. I made it through the preliminaries and was scheduled to fight Skipper Mullins for the Middleweight Championship. Skipper, who was about 6'3" with legs about six feet long, had the baby face of a teenager. He was also a good friend and had occasionally trained at my studio.

I had beaten Skipper four times in previous tournaments. After each loss he would tell me, "Next time I'm going to have a new technique." I'd laugh and retort that I would be ready for it.

Our fight on this day was scheduled to be three minutes long. The fighter with the most points at the end would be the winner. Before we went into the ring, Skipper said to me, "Why don't we just play around with each other for the first two minutes and then really try to score on each other in the last minute?" I was agreeable because I had fought some tough fighters during the days of eliminations.

When the bell rang, commencing our fight, Skipper came in with his left foot forward; he usually led with his right foot because he kicked almost exclusively with that leg. I thought he was just playing around, so I relaxed. Suddenly he blasted me with a round kick to the side of the head using his left foot—something he had never done before. It was his new technique! He had set me up again and nearly knocked me out. After I shook the cobwebs out of my head, I said, "Skipper, you son of a gun." He smiled from ear to ear. Despite Skipper's new technique, I wound up beating him again. The Grand Championship match was with Allen Steen, who had beaten me for the Grand Championship title at the Internationals in 1966. It was an extremely close fight, which I won by a decision.

*   *   *

By the end of 1967 I was the top karate fighter in America. I had won more than thirty tournaments, including the All-American Grand Championship and the Internationals, the most prestigious of all. The winner of two of the three major events becomes the Triple Crown Champion. Having achieved even more than I had ever visualized, I decided to cut down on competing and try my hand at putting on a tournament. My first attempt was to be the Las Vegas Nationals.

I had everything set up but realized it would be helpful if I could get a celebrity to endorse my tournament. While driving down the Las Vegas Strip, I saw Debbie Reynolds's name on a marquee. "I'll ask her to endorse the fight," I told Dianne. "You're dreaming," Dianne said. "She'll never endorse a karate tournament." But I believed in that old adage, "Nothing ventured, nothing gained."

I got Ms. Reynolds's manager on the telephone, introduced myself, and told him what I wanted. He took me to her suite at the hotel. I told Ms. Reynolds what I wanted, and she agreed to endorse the tournament.

We got a *gi* for Ms. Reynolds and took pictures of her with me for the cover of our program. The night before the tournament, Dianne and I went to see Ms. Reynolds perform, and she introduced me to her audience. All the publicity helped, and my tournament was a success.

As Dianne and I were leaving Las Vegas on our way home, we drove by the Aladdin Hotel, the last hotel on the Strip. Dianne wanted to try her luck at the tables. As we went into the casino, one of the pit bosses introduced himself and said he had been at the tournament. He asked whether I would consider teaching karate to him and some of the other hotel employees. I agreed and arranged to fly to Las Vegas once a week. The group soon expanded to include the children of the governor. Finally I had so many students that I decided to open a karate school in Las Vegas.

I had always believed in serendipity, the faculty of making fortunate and unexpected discoveries by accident. My experience in Las Vegas proved it. I had provoked a chain of events by getting Ms. Reynolds to endorse the tournament, thus generating needed publicity; I had gone with Dianne to the Aladdin, where the pit boss had recognized me; by agreeing to teach a select group of students, I had ended up expanding my clientele enough so that I could open another studio in an area I had never even considered. This entire chain of events had been a direct result of my decision to put on a tournament in Las Vegas.

Early in 1968 I went to Dallas to fight for the U.S. Championship. I made it to the finals along with Fred Wren, Skipper Mullins, and Joe Lewis. Fred was to be my first opponent. He was a top competitor and an aggressive fighter, so I had to be really prepared to defend myself. Texans didn't always pull their punches—despite the fact that contact was supposedly not permitted—and, in fact, our match turned into a real brawl.

In the early stages of the match I faked a low kick and

then snapped it to Fred's head, but he blocked it. While my foot was in the air, I saw his punch coming straight for my face. I thought, Oh, no, I hope he pulls it, because there was no way I could stop it. The next thing I knew I was on my back and my nose was broken. Jim Harrison, one of the line judges, jumped into the ring, grabbed my nose, and pulled it. I heard the bone crunching. Jim knew what he was doing, however. He straightened my nose out. In Dallas at that time the judges didn't penalize fighters for making contact, so Fred had scored a point.

When I got back on my feet I wasn't angry. Anger would have made me tense and affected my judgment. Instead, I became all the more determined to win. I realized that I would have to hit Fred a little harder. I didn't intend to retaliate and hit him in the face, but I knew if I didn't stop him he'd keep on me.

When we squared off again, Fred rushed in. I hit him hard in the stomach, knocking the wind out of him. He had to suck air. Bending over and gasping for breath is the most embarrassing thing in the world for a karate fighter. That gave me a point. I needed one more to win.

We went at it again. I hit Fred harder a second time in the stomach. He dropped to his knees, and the match was over.

My next fight was with Skipper, and I won. Then Joe and I fought for the championship. I had never beat Joe the same way twice, and he was as wary of me as I was of him. Neither of us was able to score in the early stages of the match.

One of Joe's favorite moves was a side kick that I usually blocked. I decided that the next time I saw the side kick coming I would drop to the floor and kick up between his legs, making light contact in the groin area. Everything worked perfectly, but since I didn't want to cause him any injury I controlled the kick and ended up just short of light contact, thus missing making the point.

We stalked each other again, and suddenly Joe closed the distance between us with incredible speed and grabbed the sleeve of my *gi*, ripping it right off my arm. He spun me around so my back was to him and then punched me in the kidney, scoring a point just as the bell rang. He had won the fight by one point.

After the match I congratulated Joe on his win. Until that time he and I had never gotten along very well because he couldn't handle losing to me. But after beating me that night he became friendly. My brother Wieland, who had matured into an excellent karate fighter, had placed second to Joe in the heavyweight division.

When I returned home from Dallas, I was extremely sore from my bruises and broken nose, which had begun to ache. I fell into bed exhausted. The next morning I awoke with a bad headache. My son Eric, who was still very young, climbed onto the bed and started jumping up and down. I was lying with my eyes shut, not paying much attention to him. Suddenly he fell and landed on top of me. His head crashed into my nose, breaking it again. I had to have it reset for the second time in two days.

* * *

Later in the year I was reminded again of a lesson learned but forgotten. I went east for a tournament. As usual, the competitors lined up and fought whoever was in line next to them. The youngster alongside me had just earned his black belt; I was to be his opponent in his first fight. He knew that I was rated number one in the country, and he was so nervous that he had to dash to the bathroom—he was sick to his stomach. Before the fight I went over and put my arm around him. "Don't worry," I said. "You'll do just fine."

When we got into the ring I still felt sorry for him and mentally planned to ease up on him. The result: he beat me. But it was my own fault. I repeated a mistake I had made in one of my first matches: I had underestimated an opponent. Of course, on any given day anyone can beat anyone else. We see that constantly in sports, when the number eighty-four seed in tennis beats the champion. The contender is relaxed, with nothing to lose, and the champion is overconfident. A true champion, however, can deal with his failures as well as his successes, and learns from both. I resolved that I would never again repeat the mistake of being overconfident.

Bruce Lee telephoned one morning in 1968. He had been signed as stunt coordinator for a film entitled *The Wrecking Crew*, starring Dean Martin, Elke Sommer, and Sharon Tate. "There's a small role in it that you'd be good for," Bruce said. "You'll play Elke Sommer's bodyguard and have one line. Are you interested?" Although I had no clue as to what acting was about, I figured I could breeze through one line. I was also excited at the prospect of working in my first film, so I enthusiastically accepted. Bruce gave me the date I was to report on the set.

Soon after that conversation, Ed Parker, promoter of the Internationals, reminded me that if I won the Internationals two years in a row I would get my name inscribed on a beautiful silver cup. Boy, I thought, I gotta get my name on that cup. I agreed to fight in his tournament, which was scheduled for the day before I was to make my acting debut.

On the day of the tournament I watched my principal rivals, Joe Lewis and Skipper Mullins, easily make it through the early rounds. Joe then was disqualified for intentionally injuring one of his opponents. Skipper won his division. This meant I would have to fight him for the title of Grand Champion.

In the locker room before the match I had a few quiet words with Skipper, who was a good friend. I leveled with him. "Skipper," I said, "I have my first part in a movie tomorrow, so beat on my body but try not to hit me in the face. I don't want to go on the set looking like I've been in a brawl."

Skipper smiled. "OK," he said. "But you'll owe me one."

I should have known better; this was the same fighter who had lulled me into a false sense of security in a previous bout and then nailed me.

Just prior to the fight, Bruce Lee brought me over to

meet Steve McQueen, who was sitting with him in the front row. I was impressed. Steve was a major film star, and he seemed as real a person offscreen as he was on. He wished me luck with the fight and on the set the next day—Bruce had obviously told him about my role. I had no idea then that in the near future Steve and I would become friends.

Skipper and I went into the ring and bowed. Skipper was famous for his kicks, but he rarely used his hands. He immediately threw a round kick, one of his favorite opening moves. I had anticipated this and blocked it, just as I had so many times before. But this time Skipper followed up with a back fist, a technique he had never used before. His move was totally unexpected, and I never even saw his fist coming. It caught me flush in the left eye. I felt the eye beginning to swell up and knew I was going to have a real shiner.

I felt anger surging through my brain, but I knew that anger is self-defeating. It would make me tense and over-anxious to score on him. Also, the damage had been done. One black eye or two—it didn't matter any longer. So I kept my cool.

Skipper had scored with his back fist and led by three points going into the third round. At that point, he kept running out of the ring, trying to stall for time. I knew I could score on him if I could only keep him in the ring long enough to make my move. While he was dancing back to stall yet again, I said, "Skipper, why don't you stay in the ring and fight like a man?"

He stopped running and came back into the ring to fight.

I beat him. Later, I told him he had been stupid—if he had kept up his delaying tactics, he would have won. Instead, he gave me a chance to beat him. But I had hurt his pride with my taunt, and he had reacted with anger and lost.

My name was inscribed on the cup! But I had something besides the cup to remind me of my win. The next day I showed up on the film set with a shiner that took a makeup man two hours to hide.

My film debut consisted of only one line of dialogue: "May I, Mr. Helm?" Dean Martin was to enter the night-club, hand me his gun, and walk to a booth. The sequence ended with a fight between us.

For the previous two weeks I had gone over and over that one line, trying to find the perfect way to deliver it. When the cameras started to roll, Dean entered on cue. As he came closer to me I could feel my throat tightening up and my body getting rigid. My one line came out in a whisper. Dean gave me the pistol, and I thought, There goes my movie career. I couldn't even say one line. Luckily the director couldn't have cared less.

Next we started on the fight scene. Dean was to be photographed in the first stage of the fight and then be doubled by Mike Stone. For the opening shot, I was to throw a spinning heel kick over Dean's head. I asked him how far he planned to drop so I could calculate how close I could kick over his head. He told me not to worry, he'd drop way down, and he bent his knees about halfway to the floor to demonstrate.

When the director called, "Action," Dean forgot to

bend his knees. I hit him flush on the shoulder and sent him flying across the set. The director was horrified, but Dean was good-natured and said, "Let's do it again."

When we did the retake I decided to kick way over Dean's head, just in case he didn't drop down far enough. But this time he sank to a squatting position on the floor. My kick went about six feet over his head.

Although I hadn't performed up to my own expectations, the scene looked fine on film. I enjoyed being in the movie, but it was not an experience I was in a hurry to repeat. I had been too tense because I was not sure of myself; I had never acted before and didn't know what to expect, so I couldn't prepare. The job did have a residual benefit, however: it got me into the Screen Actors Guild.

As a result of the publicity I had gotten from my tournament wins, I received a message from an advertising agency representing Black Belt Cologne. They were looking for a karate expert to do a commercial and wanted to see some film of me breaking something. A commercial on television was a big deal. It would give me prestige and exposure, which could help me get more students. Also, the money I was to be paid would be welcome. My senior instructor, Pat Johnson, videotaped me breaking burning cinder blocks and some boards. We sent the tape to the agency, and I was signed for the commercial. Bob Wall and Mike Stone, two of the top *karateka* in the nation, flew to New York with me to help out.

During four eight-hour days of filming, I had to break

more than three thousand roofing tiles with flying kicks. I kicked, punched, and chopped my way through four hundred boards held by Bob and Mike, who were showered by the bits and pieces. By the time the commercial was finished, I was so sick of breaking cinder blocks and boards that I never wanted to see another one of either again.

My school was prospering, and when the store next to my studio in Redondo Beach became vacant, I rented it. There was a wall between it and the dojo, but I didn't have enough money to hire a contractor to take it out. The solution was simple. I had my students practice flying kicks against the wall. In very short order, the wall was kicked down.

My plans to stop competing and devote myself to teaching were put on the back burner when, late in 1968, promoter Aaron Banks called from New York. He asked me to fight for the World Professional Middleweight title at the Waldorf-Astoria Hotel in New York. That was an important title in the pecking order of karate tournaments and a goal I had never considered. The $1,000 prize money was also a strong incentive. There was one other factor: my opponent was to be Louis Delgado, a very talented and versatile fighter who was almost ten years my junior. He had beaten me in a tournament earlier in the year. Although we were friends, I wanted to fight him again.

During the first few minutes of the match, Louis broke

my jaw with a heel kick that dropped me to my knees. My adrenaline level was so high, however, that I didn't feel any pain. We went on with the bout, and I used a judo sweep to take Louis's legs out from under him. He crashed to the mat with arms outstretched to break his fall. As I dropped down to punch him, my knee landed on his arm and broke it. I didn't know the extent of the damage, however, because Louis kept fighting until the match was over and I was declared the winner. As we rode to the hospital together, Louis and I joked about our injuries.

Although winning the pro title was satisfying, I realized again that the most exciting part of reaching one's ultimate goal was working toward it. Winning the small tournaments in the early stages of my career had been just as exciting as winning the World Championship.

Early in 1970, Bruce Lee called to say goodbye. He was going to Hong Kong to star in a movie. "I'll become a star there, and then the Hollywood producers will want me," he said. Bruce was so strongly motivated and had such determination that I felt certain he would succeed.

A few days later, my friend Larry Morales asked me to accompany him to a psychic in Redondo Beach, California. He came out of the reading enthused and persuaded me to have one too. After a few minutes of conversation, the psychic asked me if I had considered a career in movies. After my experience in *The Wrecking Crew*, I was able to truthfully say, "Never." She told me to think about it, that I would do well at it. I thought, Man, she

96

sure doesn't know me very well, or she wouldn't be saying something so ridiculous. When my reading was almost over she threw me for a loop by asking if there was anything in my house that had the shape of a half-moon. I said, "I don't think so."

As we drove to my house I told Larry that the psychic had me pegged all wrong. When I got home, however, and walked in the front door of my house, I chanced to look up at the grandfather clock in the entry hall. There, on its face was a half-moon. Whoa, I thought maybe that psychic knows something I don't know.

The single most tragic event of my life took place in 1970.

I was refereeing a demonstration match at Fumio Demura's tournament at the Japanese Deer Park in California in June when I heard a voice on the loudspeaker announce, "Chuck Norris, you have an urgent call." I rushed to a telephone. My mother-in-law, Evelyn, was crying as she blurted out the news: my brother Wieland had been killed in Vietnam.

I put the phone down, and for a moment I was numb. Dianne, who had seen my abrupt exit from the match, came in from the audience and asked me, "What's wrong?" As soon as I blurted out what I had been told, the reality of it hit me and I broke down crying. I realized that Wieland was dead and I would never see him again. I started to cry uncontrollably. My mind flooded with memories of rocking Wieland to sleep in my arms, hard times and good times shared as we were growing up, the day he earned his black belt under me. Having grown up basically without a father, we had an extremely close relationship and were sensitive to each other's needs. Wieland was also my best friend.

I learned later that he had been killed while leading his squad through Vietcong territory. He ordered his men to stop while he took the point. Wieland saw an enemy patrol laying a trap and yelled to warn the others. The Cong cut him down. He would have celebrated his twenty-eighth birthday the following month.

Aaron, who was in the army in Korea, got an emergency leave to come home for the funeral. In a way, Wieland's death brought me even closer to Aaron because there were only two of us left.

Not only had Wieland predicted some sixteen years earlier that he wouldn't live to reach the age of twenty-eight, but another strange psychic experience concerning Wieland happened to a friend of ours, and to this day I am unable to explain it.

While Wieland was in Vietnam, our friend Tony Lawrence had started writing episodes for a television series called *The Sixth Sense*. Months after Wieland was killed, Tony was driving along Hollywood Boulevard when he saw a sign in front of a store that said "Medium." Tony was always looking for new angles for the series, so he stopped, went into the darkened store, and sat down among a dozen or so other people. An elderly woman was walking around the room talking to the others.

Eventually she approached Tony and asked, "Who's Morris?"

"I don't know anybody named Morris," Tony said.

The woman got upset at Tony's response, and she left.

A few minutes later she returned. "Who is Willie?" she demanded.

"You must mean Wieland Norris," said Tony.

"Yes," she said. "He wants me to tell you that he's OK."

The hair on the back of Tony's neck stood up. He left right away.

Tony didn't tell me that story until a year and a half after Wieland was killed because he knew I was taking my brother's death pretty hard. It has taken me a long time to accept Wieland's death. Even today I have difficulty talking about it.

A true champion can deal with his failures and losses as well as with his successes, and he learns from both.

Never underestimate an opponent. You can be defeated as easily by overconfidence on your part as by his skill.

FIVE

PRISCILLA PRESLEY CALLED one day to say she wanted to study karate with me. We had been introduced by Ed Parker at a tournament. I knew that Elvis was one of Ed's black belts in kenpo-karate and asked Priscilla why she didn't study with Ed. "Ed can't teach me because he is Elvis's private trainer as well as his personal bodyguard," Priscilla explained.

Priscilla came to her first lesson wearing a *gi*. Even when she perspired she was beautiful. She worked hard, and I soon discovered she was serious about her training. I know that many people think karate is a macho endeavor, and to some extent they are right. However, there are many women competing in karate today, and they are very good. Actually, many of them are as good as men. Because of this and because of the fact that when a female is attacked her antagonist is most often a male, I don't alter my training program for women.

Priscilla usually started her lessons with stretching exercises to loosen and warm up the muscles. Then I taught her some basic kicks. Priscilla had studied ballet, which gave her an edge over many students because she was already limber and able to execute high kicks with ease. Within a month she was able to kick anywhere I directed with force and precision.

When we started free-style sparring (a free exchange of blows, blocks, and counterattacks until a cleanly executed attack to a vital point is made) I put a boxer's head-guard on her. Although most students welcome the face protection, Priscilla, although she was an actress, scorned it. "I won't have one of these on in the street," she said.

Once she even insisted on going out into the alley behind the studio to work out with high-heeled shoes, because, she said, that was what she usually wore.

Priscilla had many of the qualities I value in a person. She was open, vital, and had a positive attitude toward life. Dianne and I became friendly with her, and we occasionally flew with her to Las Vegas to watch Elvis perform.

Actually, I began teaching karate to celebrities quite by accident. Dan Blocker, a gentle giant of a man who was a star of *Bonanza*, one of the most popular television shows of the sixties, had seen me at a tournament in 1970. He asked me to come to his house and teach his children. There were five of them, each with a name beginning with *D*, including Dana, Dirk, and David. My class soon expanded to include some neighbors' kids.

Dan invited me to lunch with him at Paramount Studios, where the series was filmed, and introduced me to Michael Landon, who also starred in the series. Michael asked me to teach karate to him and David Canary, who was also in the series. Michael, who had been an Olympic-class javelin thrower, was in superb shape, as was David, who was a dancer.

Michael asked me to join him on a popular television game show called *Name Droppers*. The show consisted of guest celebrities, a panel of nine people, and contestants. The panel's job was to guess which celebrity was involved with which contestant. I was introduced as either Joanne Worley's driving instructor, Glenn Ford's son-in-law, or Michael Landon's karate instructor. The celebrities were then asked questions and, by their answers, tried to throw the panel off the track. Only one panelist picked me as the karate instructor. Most of them thought I was Glenn Ford's son-in-law.

I did a few more game shows on TV and got a call from the *Dinah Shore Show* producer asking me to demonstrate some karate. Dinah's guest was Zsa Zsa Gabor, and the producer wanted me to do something that would shock Dinah and Zsa Zsa but that would be humorous at the same time.

I worked out a little gag with Dianne, who was to be planted in the audience the day of the show.

The plan called for me to do a few karate moves and then pick someone out of the audience and show them how easy it was to learn some simple karate techniques. I finished the demonstration and went into the audience. Pointing at Dianne, I asked her to join me on the stage.

"Let's say a man has just tried to grab you," I said to Dianne. "Here's what I want you to do." I demonstrated a technique, and Dianne acted as though she didn't know what was going on. "OK," I said. "Now let's see if you can do it."

We went through it once slowly. Dianne, who was obviously nervous, kind of stumbled along. "Now let's do it for real," I said.

I started to grab Dianne, and she reacted like a whirlwind, blocking my hands, chopping me full power in the neck, punching me with all her might in the stomach, uppercutting me on the chin, side-kicking me in the stomach, and then kicking me hard in the groin. I dropped to the floor. Dinah and Zsa Zsa were in total shock, but no more than I was.

When the show was over, I asked Dianne why she had gone at me full bore instead of with light contact as we had rehearsed.

"I got so nervous I forgot what I was supposed to do," she said.

"Well, you almost killed me," I said.

Bob Barker, who had a television program called *Truth*

or Consequences, saw Dianne and me on Dinah's show. He called to ask if we would do some karate on his show. Dianne was thrilled. Not only was Bob her favorite show-business personality, but he had gone to school with her father in Mission, South Dakota.

"Let's get it right this time," I told Dianne.

We rehearsed our routine and went on Bob's show. The same thing happened again. Dianne came at me with full power, repeating what she had done before, including the punishing kick to the groin.

When I asked her later why she hadn't been able to control herself, she said, "I don't know why, but when the camera starts to roll I just fall apart. I get so nervous."

Bob was pleased with our performance, however, and asked me to come back on his show four more times. During the breaks we talked about the martial arts, and he became enthused about them. One day he asked me to teach him.

Frequently celebrities say they want to study karate when what they really want is to get some publicity or learn enough to talk about it. Bob said he was interested in karate because he wanted to stay in good physical shape and learn to defend himself. I realized Bob was sincere and agreed to teach him.

Bob was trim and strong and took to karate instantly. He studied with me three hours a week, in the morning, and became so enthusiastic that he even converted his garage into a gymnasium.

I soon found that Bob and I had a lot in common. Like me, he had grown up in a small town and married his childhood sweetheart. Despite the fact that he has been a star for so many years, he is one of the nicest people I have ever met. He is as patient and pleasant in person as he is on his show. In his case, what you see on TV is his true persona.

Dianne and I often went out to dinner with Bob and his wife, and it was a pleasure to be with them. He was a real gentleman. In all the time we spent together I never heard him say anything unkind about anyone. He even gave me the name of his business manager, who helped me sort out some of my karate schools' financial problems.

When I began making films my senior instructor, Pat Johnson, took over as Bob's instructor. Bob is expert enough in karate to be a black belt today, but he is concerned only with staying in good shape.

The manager of the Osmond family called one day to tell me that Marie, Donny, Alan, Jay, Merrill, Wayne, and Jimmy wanted to take lessons from me. I met with the entire family, including their parents. Donny said that they wanted to incorporate martial arts into their act and their upcoming TV shows, but only when I thought they were ready.

The Osmonds are probably one of the most disciplined and athletic families I have ever encountered. The wholesome quality they project on screen and stage is genuine.

The entire family was health-oriented, and each member was in excellent physical condition.

When they weren't on the road, the family studied with me three times a week. After one hour-long private lesson, most students are ready to call it quits, but the Osmonds were just beginning to warm up. Our lessons usually lasted two or three hours, but they were all so enthusiastic that I didn't object to giving them the extra time.

We usually started off with stretching exercises followed by an hour of basic blocks and combinations of kicks, including flying kicks (kicks executed while airborne). This was followed by punching techniques (any clenched-fist punch in which the force is transmitted in a straight line through the forearm to the striking point). And then we did some free-style sparring.

I impressed on them, as I do on all students, the importance of avoiding physical conflicts. I was teaching them a potentially lethal art, and I didn't want them to become involved in a situation where they might hurt another person. In time they became sufficiently self-confident that I knew they would use their martial-arts training only as a last resort.

The Osmonds had been training with me for about a year when they prepared to do a road tour. They wanted to incorporate a karate routine in their stage show and asked if I would choreograph it. The act I worked out had Donny breaking boards and Jay and Alan doing a fight scene to music.

After they had been on the road for about three weeks, I

received a telephone call from Alan. He had broken Jay's nose in the fight scene. I asked how the accident had happened. "We were getting so good at it that during each show we kept getting closer and closer with the kicks and punches," Alan said. "But one punch got too close, and there went Jay's nose."

A year later, Donny and Marie signed to do a weekly variety show called *The Donny and Marie Show*. Donny asked me to be a guest on the first episode. I agreed. Donny and I did a karate routine and *kata* (a formal exercise) in unison that led into a choreographed fight scene. That first show was a big success, and their specials were popular for years.

The family stopped studying karate when my own career interrupted their lessons. They refused to train with anyone else.

I loved teaching karate, but sometimes I had to deal with situations off the mat as well as on. For example, while teaching a class one night I noticed a husky, powerfully built man in his twenties enter the school. He sat down in a chair and pinned me with his eyes, giving off vibes of animosity. From the air of hostility surrounding him, I sensed that a problem might be looming on the horizon.

I asked one of my black belts to take over the class. I walked over to the visitor, stuck out my hand, and said, "Hi, my name is Chuck Norris." He shook hands reluctantly. I sat down next to him and said, "I'm in the middle of a class right now, but if you have any questions I'll be glad to answer them when I'm finished.''

He grunted something, and I went back to take over the class again. But his eyes never left me. When the class was over I returned to him and casually resumed our conversation.

His eyes were still cold and hostile. Mine were warm and friendly. I believe in making eye contact with people because it allows them to read you. Usually you get what you give, and I could sense his animosity slowly dissipating.

Finally he said, ''You know, you're really a down-to-earth guy, Norris. I thought you were going to be an asshole. But I'm glad to see that you're cool.'' He reached for my hand, shook it, and left.

I was certain that he had come in looking for an altercation. Had I gone over to him and said, ''What's your problem, buddy?'' there would have been one. But I have always felt that it's just as easy to make a friend as it is to make an enemy. I believe that if I can avoid a potential problem situation, life will be a lot better in all respects. If you pit negative force against negative force, there will always be a collision; even if you win, you still lose. So I always go out of my way to avoid an altercation. Having this attitude is probably the reason why, to this day, I have never had to use karate in an aggressive manner off the mat.

Very often I use humor to defuse a situation when things start coming down. For instance, when I was at a tournament in New York acting as a referee, one of the kick-boxers who was trying to make a name for himself tried to create trouble with different fighters: when they were in the ring he made loud, disparaging comments from the sidelines, and he frequently offered unsolicited advice to fighters who had lost matches.

He approached me while I was with a group and, in a voice loud enough for everyone to hear, said, "Norris, when are you and I going to fight?"

That was a deliberate public challenge, but I refused to react to it. Instead, I smiled and said, "Why do you want to pick on an old man like me?" Everyone laughed, and he moved on.

I had received enough publicity as a karate fighter by this time to attract some attention in the press, which resulted in more students and even a new relative. One evening my assistant told me that my cousin Neal Norris, from Houston, Texas, was on the phone. "I'm at Santa Monica Hospital," Neal said. "I was in town competing in a rodeo and I got hurt riding a bronc."

"I'm sorry to hear that," I said politely as I tried in vain to place him in my memory.

"I've just been discharged from the hospital," he said. "Any chance of our getting together before I leave town?"

I said that I would drop by the hospital after I finished teaching. Even after seeing Neal, I still couldn't place him, but I have a lot of cousins, so I asked him what his plans were.

"I'm going to find a cheap hotel room, spend the night, and fly home in the morning," he answered.

I invited him to spend the night at our house, and then I said I would take him to the airport.

We arrived home just as Dianne was putting Mike and Eric to bed. As soon as they learned that their cousin was a real cowboy, the boys asked if they could stay up a little longer. Neal mesmerized them with stories about his life as a bronc rider.

Dianne had just put the boys to bed and prepared the guest room for Neal when Mom called. I told her that Cousin Neal was visiting. She asked to talk with him. After about two minutes of conversation, Neal handed the phone back to me.

"I don't know who he is, but he's not your cousin," Mom said.

When I relayed the news to Dianne, she told me to get him out of the house.

"He's just a broken-down old rodeo rider," I said. "Let him spend the night and I'll drive him to the airport in the morning."

Dianne reluctantly agreed, but she insisted on bringing the boys into our bedroom for the night and locking the door. Great, I thought, now we're prisoners in our own house.

As I drove Neal to the airport, I told him that I knew he wasn't a cousin.

"You're right," he admitted, "but my last name is Norris and I feel like we really are related."

111

At the airport, Neal told me he was flat broke. I gave him twenty dollars and then left, expecting never to hear from him again.

Two hours later, while I was at the studio teaching, my brother Aaron called from the Santa Monica school. "Cousin Neal is here and I'm taking him to lunch," he said.

When I told Aaron that Neal Norris wasn't really a relative, he retorted, "Why don't you ever tell me what's going on?" Aaron ran Neal off the premises.

About a week later I began getting bills from various stores where Neal had charged clothes to me. Soon after I straightened that mess out, John Robertson called me from his school in San Diego. Cousin Neal had dropped by and signed autographs for all the students.

Is this never going to end? I asked myself. Fortunately it did, because I never heard from or about Neal again.

In 1967 Bob Wall and I went into partnership. We soon had three karate schools: one in Sherman Oaks, California, and two others in Redondo Beach. With my teaching and Bob's organizational ability, we prospered.

By the beginning of 1970 we were doing so well that a conglomerate wanting to diversify its investments offered to buy us out. Bob and I considered the offer carefully, vacillating from day to day. We were concerned that if we sold out we would end up as minority shareholders without control. On the other hand, if the conglomerate went nationwide with the schools, our small percentage of the hundreds of schools would yield profits larger than all the income from the three schools we now owned outright. We finally did sell our studios, receiving $60,000 apiece for our stock as well as a salary of $3,000 a month. I was to continue running the instruction program, and Bob would head the sales force.

On the day we got our checks, we called our wives to meet us for lunch so we could celebrate. After lunch we went directly to the bank to deposit the checks and then to Las Vegas for a real blowout.

At the time, Dianne and I were living in a very modest tract house in Torrance. One day soon after the sale, my good friend Larry Morales told me about a house on a half acre of land in Rolling Hills Estates, a nice secluded residential area with bridle paths and private streets.

Dianne went to see the house, but she wasn't enthusiastic about it. The payments would be triple what we were currently paying. When I saw the house, however, I liked it and convinced Dianne we should move because we needed the room. Also, for the first time in our lives, we had some money in the bank.

We bought the house. I used some more of the proceeds from the sale of the schools to buy a gold-color Cadillac Coupe deVille. It was the first new car we had ever owned, and was I proud of it!

There I was, at the age of thirty, a suit-and-tie executive for a major corporation. I had a big office in the Union Bank Building in Torrance, where the company had the entire top floor. I commuted in a flashy Cadillac from my big new home to the office and then to the studio where I taught classes at night. I thought I had it made. Wrong. I was setting myself up for a fall.

Many of my friends were bachelors, and I envied them their freedom to come and go when they wanted and to see whomever they pleased. Dianne and I had been married when we were just kids, and we had never been apart. I had reached a point where I didn't know whether I wanted to be married. Dianne wisely understood what I was going through and agreed to a trial separation. She took the boys to her parents' home in Florida.

It is often the case that when you get what you want, you don't want what you get. The dating game was not for me: I didn't have the time, energy, or interest for it. More important, I missed my wife and sons and what I belatedly realized was a good life. I was lonely and didn't know what to do with myself when I wasn't working. I had never before been so miserable.

It was then that Bruce Lee came back into my life. Early one morning in 1972, he telephoned from Hong Kong to say that the two pictures he had made in Hong Kong were big box-office successes. He wanted me to be in his next movie, *Return of the Dragon*, which he was also going to direct. "We'll have a fight in the Colosseum in Rome," he said. "Best of all, we can choreograph it ourselves. I promise you the fight will be a highlight of the film."

The timing was perfect. Dianne and I had been separated for four months, and I was still very depressed. Bruce was offering me an opportunity to get away from California and think my life over. Also, I was aware that an appearance in a movie—even one made in Hong Kong— could give me heightened visibility, which might draw more students to our schools. I had no thought that it might be the start of a new career for me.

Bob Wall, who also had a role in the film, was to fly with me to Rome. I arranged for us to make a one-day stopover in Florida so I could talk with Dianne about our getting back together. Dianne and my boys picked us up at the airport in the afternoon and took us back to Dianne's parents' house. After dinner, Dianne and I went for a drive and discussed what it was that we both wanted. She said, "The main issue is whether or not you want to be married." I said that after four months of being separated I had realized that I would prefer to be married. Dianne said that if I still felt the same way after I returned from making the picture we would discuss it again. Bob and I left for Rome the next morning.

When Bob and I arrived at Leonardo da Vinci Airport in Rome, Bruce was waiting with a camera crew to photograph us getting off the plane. He planned to use the shot as an insert for the film. It had been two years since I had last seen him, but Bruce was as cordial as ever. He was not embarrassed by affection, and he gave me a warm hug as he led us to a waiting car.

For the scene in the Colosseum, Bruce wanted me to look more formidable as his opponent. I weighed about

162 pounds to his 145, and he asked me to gain at least twenty pounds. Luckily, I have a very slow metabolism and can put on seven pounds in less than a week if I cut down on my workouts and don't watch my diet. I was to go on an eating binge at company expense.

Bob and I spent those first two weeks sightseeing like typical tourists. We took day-long walks, visiting such shrines as Saint Peter's, the Vatican, and the Trevi Fountain, an important location in the film *Three Coins in the Fountain*, which I had recently seen; we chased each other up and down the Spanish Steps for exercise and then bought some leather luggage at Gucci on the Via Condotti; we were awed by the catacombs and the beautiful gardens at the Villa Borghese. Between each scenic spot and ancient historical monument I hunted for a restaurant where I could load up on pasta and Italian ice cream, the best I had ever tasted. Almost every night we ate at the Tavernia Flavia in Trastevere. In fact, when I returned to Rome some years later on a promotion tour for a film, I went to the restaurant and renewed some old friendships.

I got heavy enough on schedule, and Bruce and I went to the Colosseum to block out the action. It was an eerie feeling standing with Bruce in one of the tunnels leading out into the arena. I was reminded of movies like *Spartacus*, in which Kirk Douglas fought in the arena. But the Colosseum was much more impressive and much larger than I had ever imagined. It dawned on me that, not so long ago, gladiators had gone out there to fight to the death before a cheering crowd.

We talked the scene through as Bruce took notes on camera angles. Bruce planned our scene as though we were two gladiators pitted against each other. Since we were doing our own choreography, Bruce would ask me, "What do you want to do?" I demonstrated the techniques that I thought would be interesting, and he worked out his defenses. Then he attacked me, and I worked out my moves. It took us only one long day to put the fight scene together, since we had worked out with each other so often and knew each other's moves so well.

Our fight scene, which was to come at the climax of the picture, took three days to film. It was difficult and challenging but fun to work with Bruce. Despite being a novice director, he knew what he wanted and how the camera operator should photograph it. I played the heavy in the picture, but luckily Bruce, being a friend, didn't make me out to be that bad a figure. When his character killed mine, he put my uniform and belt over me very ceremoniously and with respect. *Return of the Dragon* cost only $240,000 to make; ultimately it was to earn more than eighty million dollars worldwide. The fight between Bruce and me did indeed become a classic, as he had promised.

After filming the fight scene, Bruce, Bob Wall, and I flew to Hong Kong to complete our other scenes. On the day we arrived there, Bruce arranged for all of us to be guests on the most famous local TV show, *Enjoy Yourself Tonight,* Hong Kong's version of Johnny Carson's show.

We were questioned about the movie, and I was asked

to demonstrate some karate. I started by kicking a cigarette out of Bob's mouth. Then Bob and I sparred a little to show our style.

The next day, in a local paper, someone challenged me to a fight. Bruce, who read Chinese, was amused by the story and read it to me. "Forget about it," he said, "I am constantly being challenged. It's a no-win situation. All this guy wants is publicity." Nevertheless, Bob was upset. "I'm not starring in the movie," he said to Bruce. "How about me accepting?" "No problem there," Bruce said. So it was arranged for Bob to go on the show the next night. He told the viewing audience, "My instructor, Chuck Norris, has been challenged by a viewer. Now Chuck is a much better fighter than I am, so I want you, whoever you are, to fight me first to see if you qualify to face him. Our fight will be held on this show so everyone in Hong Kong can see it, because I'm going to beat you to death right here."

Of course the character, whoever he was, never showed up, and I was never again challenged in Hong Kong.

Bruce lived well. He had bought a big house in the most exclusive section of Kowloon and had staffed it with servants. He had even ordered a specially built red Mercedes Benz from Germany. His wife, Linda, was with him, busy raising their son, Brandon, and daughter, Shannon. Despite the fact that they had an excellent chef, Linda insisted on doing the cooking when Bob and I occasionally visited them for dinner.

I had called Dianne a few times while I was in Rome

and Hong Kong. The separation had made me realize all the more how much I loved my wife and children. I wanted them back. But Dianne was noncommittal. She was having a good time in Florida, she said, and the boys were fine. Although Bob was with me, I was still lonely and unhappy.

On an afternoon off, Bob and I went to see *On Any Sunday*, a motorcycle-racing documentary starring Steve McQueen. When the film was over, I told Bob that McQueen was the one actor I really would like to know, because I admired him so much. He was my kind of man, a doer. He radiated a certain strength and macho image, and I knew he raced cars as well as motorcycles.

I didn't mention my admiration of McQueen to Bruce, however. Their friendship had dimmed over the years because Bruce considered himself to be in competition with Steve as a box-office draw. I told Bruce that I believed his comparing himself to Steve or anyone else was a negative thing to do. "By doing that you subconsciously place yourself beneath that person, and your conscious mind will take it for a fact," I said. "Surpassing Steve should not be your goal. The only thing that really matters is what you accomplish yourself."

Bruce wasn't having any of my philosophy, however. He said his dream was to be a bigger star than Steve, and that was one of the reasons he had gone to Hong Kong. He intended to become a top star in the Orient, which he felt would make him more in demand for American films.

When I returned home from Hong Kong I telephoned

Dianne every day. She came to L.A. for the wedding of a cousin, and we talked. I literally begged her to come back to me, but her answer was a firm no. When she went back to Florida I kept up the phone calls and sent flowers and letters almost daily.

It was about this time that I received word that my father had been killed in a car accident in Oklahoma. I sent a telegram to Aaron, who arranged for an emergency leave and flew in from Korea to meet me for the funeral in Wilson, Oklahoma. I learned that my father had cancer. Part of his throat and chin had been removed, and a tube had been inserted in his trachea to help him breathe. He had been thrown out of his car in the wreck, and the tube had come out. He died on the ground of suffocation because no one at the accident site was aware of the tube.

It was a sad time for Aaron and me; we were mourning a man we scarcely knew, even though he was our father. After we took care of the funeral arrangements, I flew home and Aaron went back to Korea.

I finally convinced Dianne that, for the sake of our children, she should give our marriage another try. From then on I worked 110 percent at my marriage. It was rocky at first. After a year, however, everything between us was again fabulous. We were closer than ever before.

It's just as easy to make a friend as it is to make an enemy. If you are hostile, expect a hostile response from others. Whatever you project is what you will usually receive in return.

Surpassing another person should not be your goal. The only thing that really matters is what you accomplish yourself.

SIX

I WAS ABOUT to start a class one day in 1972 when the telephone rang. "This is Steve McQueen," the caller said. "I'd like to bring my son, Chad, in for lessons." I suspected someone was putting me on, although the voice sounded familiar.

I suggested that Steve and his son come by the studio in Sherman Oaks the next day. Although I had sold the school, I still worked out and taught my private students there.

At the appointed time I heard a motorcycle roar up the street. I'd said nothing about the call to anyone because I wasn't certain whether McQueen would actually show up. One of my black belts was standing by the window, and he turned to me and said, "Damned if it isn't Steve McQueen coming here."

Steve came in wearing his motorcycle gear, followed by Chad, dressed almost identically. Both of them were carrying helmets.

We all shook hands. "Bruce introduced me to you some time ago at a tournament," Steve said. "He told me if I ever wanted to take karate lessons, you were the best."

It turned out that Chad had been in a fight in school and Steve wanted him to learn how to defend himself. Chad was about seven years old and seemed to be a fine young man, and I was especially impressed with Steve, who lived up to my expectations: he was a no-nonsense type of man who got directly to the point.

Steve came to a few of Chad's lessons and then told me he himself would like to take private lessons. Steve took to karate quickly because he had excellent reflexes and natural athletic ability. He trained hard and was a born fighter, not afraid to mix it up with anybody. Once he made up his mind to do something, he went all out.

His biggest problem in training was his lack of flexibility. He was not very limber and had difficulty executing high kicks. Ali MacGraw, his wife, invited Steve and me to join her at her exercise class in Beverly Hills. When we arrived, Shirley Jones and Susan Dey, stars of television's *The Partridge Family,* were already there. Ron Fletcher, the instructor, gave Steve and me a pair of flimsy skintight leotards to wear. One pair was pink and the other blue. I grabbed the blue pair. We went into the locker room to change clothes. To say we looked ridiculous in those outfits would be an understatement. In addition, the leotards left nothing to the imagination. Steve said, ''Damned if I'm going out there looking like this.''

''Let's just walk out there and act like we've been doing this forever,'' I said.

''OK,'' said Steve reluctantly, and he went out of the dressing room first in his pink leotard. As soon as he stepped out of the door I held it shut so he couldn't come back in.

I shut the door after him and locked it. I knew he had heard the door lock, because he returned and began to pound on it, but I refused to let him in. I figured that after the girls got tired of looking and laughing at him they wouldn't pay any attention to me.

A few minutes after I heard the laughter subside I left the dressing room and found Steve in the studio sitting on the floor and talking to the women. I casually walked over and sat down next to him. I was right. The only one who even looked at me was Steve. If looks could kill, I'd have been dead!

The class was fun for me because I was already limber, but Steve complained about my trickery and his stiffness for days afterward.

Such shared adventures helped us become friendly, although we never became real friends. Steve was very self-centered and not an open kind of person. He suffered a paranoia common to many actors: he feared that people were always trying to take advantage of him because he was a star. Such thoughts concerned him so much that he once asked me how I knew who my real friends were.

"The only one who suffers from that kind of thinking is you," I said. "If you enjoy someone's company, then you shouldn't wonder about his ulterior motives."

One of the few arguments Steve and I ever had was early in 1973, when he was doing a movie called *The Towering Inferno*. A friend of mine from out of town came to Hollywood for a visit. I asked Steve if I could bring him to the set. Steve promised to leave my name at the studio gate. When we arrived at the studio the guard said my name wasn't on the visitors list, and no one was allowed on the set. Naturally I was confused and embarrassed.

I called Steve the following morning and asked what had happened. Steve said he had changed his mind about having us on the set. He didn't know what motives my friend had for wanting to see him. I thought that was pretty ridiculous and said so. I told Steve that he would lose a lot of friends with that attitude. I chided him for putting me on the spot, and he apologized.

That wall Steve had built around himself precluded personal conversations, so we talked mainly about racing, motorcycles, cars, and karate. We liked each other and respected each other's abilities, but we rarely socialized together or went out with both of our wives.

After a workout one day we left the Sherman Oaks dojo together and saw a fresh layer of cement around a parking meter on the street. Steve found a stick, bent over, and wrote, "Steve and Ali." I followed suit and wrote, "Chuck and Dianne." The messages are still there in the cement.

Ali was a beautiful and delightful person. For Easter,

she hand-painted a really exquisite egg that she gave Dianne and me as a gift. In return, we gave the McQueens two rabbits.

Steve taught my two sons how to ride motorcycles, with the stipulation that they ride them only in the country and never on the street. I rode in the pillion seat on his cycle several times; it was a treat because he was a superb cyclist with excellent control.

On my return from making the film in Hong Kong with Bruce, I found my business affairs in shambles. The company that had bought the schools had no notion of how to operate a personal service business in which decisions have to be made immediately. My partner, Bob Wall, and I tried to tell them what they were doing wrong. We knew we had to get back into the end of the business where we had made our success in the first place: supervising and encouraging students and developing new ideas and techniques. We couldn't do that from an office, and the company didn't want us in the field. Because we were minority stockholders, they refused to listen to us. Bob finally got fed up and went into the real-estate business.

By 1973 the owners of our schools were in deep financial trouble and had lost more than a million dollars. They sold the schools to another group, which, in turn, sold them to an individual who was more interested in siphoning off the assets than in increasing the income. This man told me he would be bankrupt within a few months.

I didn't want the schools that boldly carried my name to

be associated with bankruptcy, so I asked him how much was owed. He said he was $140,000 in debt. "You take over the debts, and you can have the remaining seven schools," he told me. I made the deal with him. Because of my lack of business experience, I neglected to include in the contract a clause saying that I would be responsible only for those debts I had been told about.

I sat down with a notepad and figured out that if I sold five of the schools for $25,000 apiece, that would bring in $125,000. I had a little money saved that would make up the difference. I could still keep two schools.

I contacted my black belts, who were already running five of the schools. I asked each one whether he wanted to buy the school he was managing. They each agreed to put $5,000 down and pay me off at $500 a month. Dianne ran the finance company and kept the books.

I then called each creditor. I explained the situation and told them I didn't want to go into Chapter 11. I promised to personally pay them a hundred cents on the dollar if they would give me time. Most of them were amazed at this offer. If the schools declared Chapter 11, I would only have to pay ten cents on every dollar owed. I reiterated that I didn't want my name on a bankruptcy proceeding. They agreed to let me pay them off, dividing the $2,500 I got each month from my black belts between them.

The black belts made regular payments, and everything went smoothly until I was suddenly hit with an additional $120,000 in bills, including payroll, state, and federal taxes the previous owners had neglected to tell me about.

If I didn't pay $12,000 immediately, the state would close all the schools.

I went to a businessman friend of mine, showed him the books, and asked for his advice. "Go into bankruptcy," he said. "You don't have a chance to bail out of this."

I told him that Dianne and I had bought a new house that we didn't want to lose. He said I had no choice.

I was completely broke. I had personal resources but no financial resources. By borrowing from friends and relatives and even my kids' savings, I finally scraped together $11,000. But I still needed $1,000. I was desperate.

When I told Bob Wall about my problem, he said he didn't have any cash but he did have a $1,000 line of credit on his American Express card. He borrowed the money from it. Although I had no idea how I could pay off the loan at the end of the month, I took the money.

Meanwhile, I had to move out of my office. My friend Larry Morales came by to help. He brought a pickup truck and a couple of employees. I mentioned to Larry that I had four desks that I wanted to sell for a hundred dollars apiece. Larry said he knew someone who might be interested and took the desks away with him. Two hours later he returned with $400. I asked who had bought the desks. Larry said it was someone who had a large machine shop.

A couple of months later I went to visit Larry. As I walked around his machine shop I looked up in his attic and saw my four desks stored there. I realized that he had bought them himself to help me out. If he had been the owner of a thriving business, this wouldn't have been a big deal, but Larry was just starting his new business and he was hard-pressed just to make ends meet.

Friendships are based on such gestures as Bob's and Larry's. They both came through when I needed them, and I have never forgotten it. It gives me pleasure to know that, today, both of my old friends are successful businessmen on their own.

After paying the taxes I had to call the creditors, explain the situation, and ask whether they would allow me to pay them less money each month. Again they agreed to cooperate.

I finally had to sell my last two schools. Every cent from those sales went to pay off the creditors. I also had to sell my new Cadillac.

Meanwhile, I gave seminars and taught private lessons to meet our own personal overhead. I was determined to hold on to the new house for as long as possible, but I still wasn't making enough money to cover all our expenses. Dianne kept running the finance company on her own, keeping the payments coming in on schedule. Although it was a full-time job without pay, she never complained. The pressure on us was heavy, but it didn't cause any stress between us because we were too busy trying to make things work.

In any event, I have never been able to understand the process of worrying. My belief is that when you worry your creative senses become clogged, and you are unable to see the situation clearly. I consider worry to be wasted energy. In my view, the best thing you can do when faced with a problem is not to worry about it, but to get the job done the best way you can. There were moments during that low period when I started to feel depressed, but I'd always regroup and say to myself, Hey, get your act together.

One night I asked Dianne, "What's the worst that can happen? We'd just have to start over again. Is that really so bad, when you look around and see the problems other people face, problems that make ours seem minuscule?"

She agreed. Then an amazing thing happened. Just prior to my selling the last two schools, the producers of *The Tonight Show* called. They wanted to know about one of my students. His name was Phil Paley, and he was the youngest black belt in America. Phil was a handsome towheaded nine-year-old who was small for his age but exceptionally good at karate. We were invited onto the show, and we did a demonstration after which Johnny Carson came out on stage and participated, allowing Phil to throw him around.

Bill Marr, a prominent businessman in Norfolk, Virginia, who owned the Yellow Cab Company there, as well as several other businesses, happened to watch the show. He telephoned me the next day to say that his young son was taking karate from a Korean instructor and that he was interested in buying a karate-school franchise. I didn't know what that really entailed, and since he was just coming out to inquire I didn't consider it a big deal. On the day Bill arrived I was giving a seminar, which turned out to be fortunate because instead of seeing me he met

131

with Pat Johnson, who was able to sell me and our system far better than I could have.

Pat explained our belief that when a person says he wants to learn karate, he is really saying, "Make me a better person." We realized that it's the positive concepts the student develops within himself that make him feel better about himself. If someone feels good about himself physically, that will transfer into a better mental attitude, and we motivated our students to work hard in each area. At the same time we tried to instill a philosophical approach to life that would be of general all-around benefit.

We knew that after a while kicking and punching get boring. There has to be more to a lesson than that to make the student want to return. Ours was a well-rounded system that not only made for better fighters but also made people feel happier about themselves. As a result, we had a very low attrition rate.

Bill said he was interested in our concepts, but first he intended to check out other schools around the country. He promised to call us if he wanted to strike a deal. Two months later he contacted us and said that he preferred our system to the others he had investigated. He wanted to meet with us again and talk about buying a franchise.

Bill returned to Los Angeles and met with me. Just like that, he bought a franchise. My brother Aaron and Rick Prieto went to Virginia Beach to open the schools and stayed with them for five years. They inspired and motivated their students so well that the schools immediately flourished. Today, Bill Marr's two schools in Virginia are the most successful karate schools in the world. He now has his own two-story building with 24,000 square feet of training space.

He had no way of knowing it then, but the money he paid for the franchise in 1973 kept me and Dianne going for the next several years.

Those years were the most trying period of my life. Everything I had worked so hard to achieve seemed to be going down the drain. But I received several benefits from those hard times. For one thing, I discovered that I was naive about business. For another, the problems brought Dianne and me even closer together because we functioned as a team. And I reconfirmed my belief that if you feel deep in your heart that you can accomplish something—no matter how impossible it seems—you can if you are determined and persistent enough.

I overcame a situation that would have daunted many businessmen, solely because I believed that everything would work out for the best—and it did. In time, I was able to pay back the creditors every cent I owed them. When I saw the businessman who had advised me to go bankrupt, he said he would have bet me a thousand dollars to a donut that I could not have done it.

Never think to yourself, I can't do this. Your subconscious takes you at your word, and you won't be able to succeed. Think positively, and your subconscious will help you succeed.

When faced with a problem, don't worry about it. Worry is wasted energy. Get the job done the best way you can.

133

Mom, Dad, and I when I was two years old.

Here I am with my younger brother Aaron, 1953.

I always wanted to be a cowboy in the movies!

With my brother Wieland, 1961.

Dianne and I on our wedding day,
December 29, 1958.

Relaxing Sunday visit with my
stepdad, George Knight, 1966.

Defeating Steve Sanders,
lightweight, at the International
Grand Championship, 1967.

Training camp with some of my first black belts, 1966.
My brother Wieland is fifth from the left.
(I'm third from the left.)

All-American Grand
Championship, New York, 1967.

Defeating Joe Lewis, heavyweight, at
the International Grand
Championship, 1967.

With my beloved Granny, 1971.

Defeating Louis Delgado in the National
Tournament of Champions, Washington, D.C., 1968.

As defending Grand Champion, I fought Skipper Mullins to
win the title again. International Grand Championship,
1968.

Captain of the undefeated team, Mainland vs. Hawaii, 1968.
I defeated the Hawaii state champion.

My famed spinning back kick.

Spinning crescent kick.

With the great Bruce Lee.

In *Forced Vengeance,* I played Josh Randall, a casino security chief who uses his martial-arts mastery to combat the underworld.

Lone Wolf McQuade is a favorite film among many of
my fans.

Colonel James Braddock returns to Vietnam to fight his own war in
Missing in Action.

Drawing a crowd in *Code of Silence*. That's my brother Aaron getting hit.

Armed as Matt Hunter, America's only chance of
stopping a foreign attack in *Invasion U.S.A.*

Lou Gossett, Jr., and I know we're on the right path when we discover a bejeweled dagger in *Firewalker*.

With Lee Marvin in *The Delta Force*.

My visit with President Reagan and the First Lady.

With Mom, Dad, and Aaron.

Celebrating our twenty-five years together.

My family today: with Dianne and our sons, Mike and
Eric.

The secret of inner strength has brought success and happiness to my life.

SEVEN

BRUCE LEE CAME to Los Angeles in mid-July 1973. "I'm only here for the day," he told me on the telephone. "Any chance of us meeting for lunch?" I was delighted to hear from him and curious to learn what had brought him to Los Angeles for such a short visit.

We met in Chinatown at Bruce's favorite restaurant. He appeared to be his customary ebullient self. Over the usual meal of *dim sum* he told me that he had mysteriously passed out a couple of times while making a movie in Hong Kong. The doctors there hadn't been able to come up with a satisfactory explanation, so he had decided to come to Los Angeles for a complete physical checkup. He had received the results only that morning.

"I passed with flying colors," he announced proudly.

"The doctor said I had the insides of an eighteen-year-old boy."

"What did he think caused you to pass out?" I asked.

"He didn't know. Probably overwork and stress."

Bruce went on to tell me that as a result of the success of his films plus the enthusiastic reception of *Enter the Dragon,* which was soon to be released, he had offers to make films from Warner Brothers, Carlo Ponti, and several other producers. "They're offering me blank checks for my next movie," he said. "Imagine it, I can fill in any amount I want if I'll just sign with them."

Bruce laughed delightedly and tossed a piece of Peking duck into the air with his chopsticks and neatly caught it. He offered it to me. I took it and popped it into my mouth.

He was justifiably excited about the future and said that it wouldn't be long before he was a superstar, bigger than Steve. "You watch," he said, "I'm going to become the first Chinese film star to become internationally famous."

I knew what obstacles he had overcome and how hard he had worked to get to the point he had reached, and I was happy for him. We spoke for a moment about how a man's life is built not on his years but on his accomplishments. It was a prophetic conversation that I would soon have occasion to recall.

Bruce flew back to Hong Kong. Four days later, on July 20, 1973, I heard on the news that he had died. I couldn't believe it. A friend of mine in Hong Kong told me that Bruce's death was mysterious and was being investigated.

Later I read that the Hong Kong coroner's official verdict was "death by misadventure," caused by a hypersensitive reaction to a headache-tablet ingredient. There were instantly rumors that the coroner's verdict was a coverup. The rumor given the most credence was that Bruce had deliberately been given a mortal blow by a hired killer expert in ancient Oriental assassination techniques. The killer had reportedly been hired by one of the many people whom Bruce had supposedly offended in Hong Kong. Such rumors abound when someone as physically perfect and healthy as Bruce dies so young. He was only thirty-two years old.

Bruce was in perfect physical condition when he died, and no cause of death could be readily ascertained. Governmental authorities in Hong Kong insisted that an autopsy be performed. Because of that, the media began to speculate on the cause of his death. Everyone had his own opinion, ranging from some secret martial-arts technique used by ancient assassins to poisoning, brain tumor, drug abuse—you name it.

The eventual inquest took nine days and was painstaking in its thoroughness. Finally the Hong Kong coroner made his report: "Death by Misadventure." Cause of death: cerebral edema (accumulation of fluid causing abnormal pressure on the brain). Cerebral edema can be caused by the body's allergic (hypersensitive) reaction to a substance introduced into the system. Some people have such fatal reactions to penicillin or bee stings. In Bruce's case, it was determined that his body had reacted in this manner to meprobamate, a headache-tablet ingredient.

Bruce had always pushed himself hard and never let himself relax, which probably caused the headaches for which he took medication.

More than twenty thousand grieving fans gathered at his funeral service in Hong Kong. Bruce was buried in Seattle, Washington, in a peaceful and natural setting overlooking the University of Washington, where, as a student, he had met his wife, Linda.

A memorial service was also held in San Francisco. I went there with Steve McQueen and James Coburn, who had been one of Bruce's students as well as a good friend. Jim delivered a touching eulogy. Then we all flew back to Los Angeles together, silent in our own thoughts.

I remembered my last conversation with Bruce and wondered if he had had a foreboding about his death. During his short life span, however, Bruce had accomplished what he wanted most: to be renowned as a martial artist and actor. Tragically, he had left behind a wonderful wife and two young children. The irony was that he never lived to enjoy the success and fame that came as a result of *Enter the Dragon*. Only after his death did Bruce become a legend and a bigger box-office star than Steve McQueen.

I officially retired from karate in 1974, after winning most of the major titles then available, including that of World Professional Middleweight Champion. I had ceased actively competing in 1970, when I became disenchanted with karate because of the diminishing level of sportsmanship in the competitions. Contestants began to challenge referees and judges. Instructors were getting involved, trying to control matches. In the past, if respect was not demonstrated in the ring, players were removed. To my dismay, I realized that I was witnessing a complete deterioration of the friendly competitive spirit that had built up the martial arts in America.

The last straw came when I was the guest of a promoter at a tournament. I was asked to referee one of the black-belt matches because the referee scheduled to officiate had turned out to be the instructor of one of the fighters. I reluctantly agreed. As I was refereeing the match, the student of the displaced referee executed a punch that I did not feel was worthy of a point. The instructor came running into the ring screaming, demanding to know why I hadn't given his student the point. I calmly explained my reasons. The instructor raged out of the ring, and the match continued. The opposing fighter scored a good solid point that I called. Again, the instructor came storming into the ring, haranguing me. I took as much of this as I could and then said to him, ''OK. I'll tell you what we'll do. You and I will fight, and we'll let your student referee.'' At this point the promoter came over and kept the dispute from going any further. But I realized that the tournament circuit could only suffer if this attitude continued.

I was right. The tournament scene suffered for years, until, in the early 1980s, the promoters started enforcing proper conduct and respect again. Since then, tournaments have begun to flourish again.

* * *

A few months after my official retirement I started to get bored and restless. I was without direction; I had no new challenges. I went to dinner with Steve McQueen one night and told him of my problem.

"Why don't you try acting?" he asked me.

"You must be kidding," I said, "I've never done anything that requires acting, not even a high school play."

"Acting in films is much more than just being an actor," Steve said. "It requires a presence on the screen. Only the camera can determine whether you've got that, but I suggest you try it."

I thought about what he had said for a few months and did some research. At that time there were about sixteen thousand unemployed actors in Hollywood.

When I relayed that statistic to Steve, he grinned. "Remember that philosophy of yours that you always stressed to students: set goals, visualize the results of those goals, and then be determined to succeed by overcoming any obstacles in the way. You've been preaching this to me for two years, and now you're saying there's something you can't do."

I realized that he was right. If you believe strongly enough in something, regardless of what it is, you should put your heart and soul into achieving it.

"OK," I said. "Since you put it that way, I'm going to go for it."

I discussed this conversation with Dianne. Luckily she was as supportive of me as ever, and we agreed that I should go all the way. I didn't know how to begin and finally decided to look for an acting coach.

I checked around and found that acting schools were expensive. In the yellow pages, I noticed that Estelle Harmon accepted students on the GI Bill. I enrolled in one of her classes. It was a full-time school, with classes held six to eight hours a day. These included instruction in voice, reading comprehension, and movement as well as in acting.

Most of the other students had studied acting in high school or college or had some other form of training. I was thirty-four at the time and one of the oldest students in the school. I felt like a white belt again, but I was determined to learn as much as I could.

At my first session, Estelle asked me to read a scene with an actress in which we played a husband and wife having an argument. I was rigid with fear. After class, Estelle took me aside and said, ''For an athlete, you're the stiffest person I have ever seen.'' I admitted that I had never been so scared in my life. Actually, I had no idea how difficult acting was.

During one class, Estelle said that each of us was to get up in front of the class and sing and pantomime a song. Eight of the fifteen students performed while I sat despondent in the audience and frantically tried to think of a song I knew. When it was my turn I walked to the front of the class. I was about to say I didn't know any songs when, all of a sudden, I remembered ''Dear Hearts and Gentle People.'' It was the same song I had sung as a child with my mother and brothers. I pretended I was taking off my clothes and stepping into the shower and singing. I have no idea how my voice sounded but I do remember that when I finished, I felt a great sense of accomplishment.

Earlier, Estelle had spoken to us about recalling powerful emotions from our past and drawing on them to recreate similar emotions. This was my first experience with that technique, and I realized that it actually worked. Years later I would recall some of those lessons with gratitude.

As part of each class session, students would perform excerpts from plays. Everyone would read for the various parts, and then the students would pick the classmates they thought best for the roles. I was never chosen for a single one of these roles, although I did keep performing in class.

After each student did an exercise Estelle usually asked another student to critique it. Sometimes the criticism was unbelievably harsh. I didn't believe in that kind of appraisal. It was my opinion that an actor performing in a scene wears his heart on his sleeve. I also felt that criticism should be positive rather than negative. When I was asked to critique a performance I always started with the positive aspects and then slipped in suggestions for improvement. But I never told an actor he had done something wrong, because I don't think there's a ''wrong'' way in acting. It's a matter of choices, and some are better than others.

Toward the end of the year I did a scene that I thought was quite good. Estelle chose a student to critique it. He tore my performance apart from beginning to end in a very negative and hostile way. He wanted to know what made me think I could be an actor. I felt the blood boiling inside me. Finally I looked at him and said, "Why don't you shove it? Who are you to tell me what's right and wrong? You have no more experience than I do. You might have done it a different way, but you can't say that what I did was wrong."

Then I looked at Estelle. "Estelle, I'll take criticism from you because you're qualified. But this person is not a professional actor, and I'm not going to take it." That was the last time I went to class.

Although I was aware of my lack of experience, I was still determined to follow Steve's suggestion and become an actor. First I had to decide what kind of character I wanted to play on the screen, using as much of my own persona as possible.

During the decade I had been teaching karate I had always tried to set a positive example for my students. That seemed to me to be a good basis for the character I might play. I began to build from there. I am by nature quiet, a man who has strong principles and tries hard to succeed. I could further develop this character into a man who uses his karate ability in the fight against violence.

I had in mind the Western heroes of my youth, men like John Wayne and Gary Cooper who put their guns away only to take them up again reluctantly to fight against injustice. As a child, I had sat spellbound during the early stages of these men's films, waiting impatiently for them to turn the tables on their antagonists. When they finally did, I would jump up in my seat with excitement. They were my role models during childhood, when I grew up essentially without a father. They were also my role models as a would-be actor.

There weren't many heroes of that type on the screen in the 1970s, and I felt that kids needed this kind of positive image. Perhaps I could become a role model for today's youth.

Once I had a mental image of the type of character I wanted to play, the next question was, how was I going to get the chance to do it? Since the death of Bruce Lee, producers no longer felt that karate movies would be profitable. If I waited for a producer to come and knock on my door, I knew I might be waiting a very long time. I decided I would have to make my own break and come up with my own idea for a film.

After a workout one night, I mentioned to a few of my black belts that I needed a plot for a karate movie that could be made inexpensively. John Robertson, who was one of my first black belts, spoke up. He said he had an idea for a story about the Black Tigers, an elite squadron of special commandos in Vietnam. As the war is winding down and peace negotiations with the Vietcong are underway, the squadron is called back for one last mission. It sounded fine to me, so we spent the next few days writing an outline. Neither of us had ever written a screenplay, however, and I didn't have the money to hire a writer. Finally Joe Fraley, a writer friend of mine, agreed to write the script on speculation. That meant he would be paid only if it sold.

The next step was to find someone to put up the money to make the film. I didn't go to my celebrity students for help. I was determined to do this on my own. That was the whole point of it for me: I wanted the sense of accomplishment, of winning on my own. For instance, Steve McQueen worked hard in the dojo. He had tremendous dedication once he put his mind to something, a real championship attitude. But when he slacked off or wasn't doing something right, I really came down on him. I didn't favor him in the dojo because he was a star, and I didn't expect him to do unusual favors for me that I hadn't earned just because I was his instructor. I contacted friends outside of karate who arranged for me to meet with producers.

I went to meeting after meeting, but the people I met with all had preconceptions about me. They categorized me as an athletic star who couldn't do anything but fight. Because I didn't have any acting credentials I was unable to make them realize that I could offer more to a movie than my karate skills. Also, I was insecure and nonassertive. I'd had some experience as a karate champion selling lessons to prospective students, but I hadn't had any experience selling myself as an actor. Of course, the producers immediately picked up on my tentativeness. At the end of each meeting I was always asked, ''Why do you think this movie will make money?'' I never had an appropriate answer.

I had visualized some of the obstacles that would face me, but not all of them. I was not discouraged, but I was disheartened. Meanwhile, Lo Wei, a Chinese director, asked me to play a role in a movie he was making in San Francisco called *Yellow-Faced Tiger*. He assured me it would be shown only in Hong Kong. Dan Ivan, a friend of mine, told me he had a role in it. I decided to take Dianne and the boys on an expense-paid holiday in San Francisco while I did the film.

On the day I showed up on the set, Lo Wei was handing out parts to various martial artists on a hit-or-miss basis. There was no script, and when I went up for the role I had no idea of what I was to do. Lo Wei told me I was to play the Mafia boss of San Francisco and wear a hat and smoke a cigar. I told him I don't smoke. That didn't matter to him. They bought me a cheap suit and a stogie that was about two feet long. I chewed the cigar unlit. My scenes called for me to try to rape my brother's girlfriend and be beaten up.

One night while we were in San Francisco Dianne and I decided to take the kids to a movie. While looking at the film listings in the paper I noticed an ad for a film called *The Student Teachers*. I remembered that a couple of years earlier I had received a call from an independent production company producing a film with that title. They wanted me to bring some of my students to a park in Inglewood, California, where I would conduct a karate class with two of the stars.

The producers had told me that the movie was about teachers who were unhappy with the teaching methods in schools and broke off with the system. It had all sounded innocent enough, so I had brought my two young sons, my brother Aaron, and about twenty other students to Inglewood. We had spent a balmy afternoon shooting a scene in which I taught the two stars and my students karate moves on the grass. That was it. I never heard anything else about it. But now it was playing in San Francisco.

I suggested to Dianne that we all go to the movie because Mike and Eric might enjoy seeing themselves on the screen and I was also curious. The theater was in a run-down, tough section of the city. When we arrived, Dianne said, "I'm not going to a movie here." I said, "Let's just go in and see our part and leave." Dianne agreed. The inside of the theater was worse than the outside. There were only a handful of people in the audience when we took our seats. The opening scene of the film was of a naked woman lying on a bed. Dianne and I covered the kids' eyes. "Let's get out of here," Dianne said.

By then the naked woman was off the screen. "Let's wait a few minutes longer," I said. "It can't get any worse." But it did! The sex scenes were a hard "R" and we were constantly hiding the kids' eyes. Finally our scene came on. There I was, filling the screen in a gigantic close-up. Oh, no, I thought, the one time I don't want to be on screen, and here I am, bigger than life.

Soon after we returned to Los Angeles, I was asked by a small independent production company to star in *Breaker! Breaker!*, an exploitation movie about a trucker who uses his Citizen's Band radio and the help of other truckers to thwart a corrupt judge in a speed-trap town. The title comes from the phrase "Breaker! Breaker!" used by truckers when they call for help on their CB radios.

I thought it might be a good break-in role for me as an actor. Equally important, I was to be paid $10,000 for the role, and we needed the money. Dianne and I were just barely meeting our monthly bills with my income from teaching. Although I was the star of the film, the promotional material didn't mention me, and it never played in Los Angeles. In fact, Dianne and I had to fly to San Francisco with my friend Larry Morales, who was also in the film, in order to see it. There were only two other people in the audience that Monday night. That took the excitement out of it, although the film wasn't all that bad.

For three years I knocked on doors all over Hollywood, carrying the script of *Good Guys Wear Black* and utilizing every contact I had. One day I told my accountant about the problems I was having getting the script made into a movie. He said he had a client named Allen Bodoh who was a producer and might be interested. He gave me Allen's phone number. I was all set to call, but when I found out that Allen was only in his twenties I lost my enthusiasm. What could a young kid like that know about raising money and producing films?

Months later, while visiting Larry Morales in his machine shop, I told him that I was at my wit's end—I had pitched every producer who would see me. Then I remembered Allen Bodoh and told Larry about him. "I'll call him for you," Larry said. He got Allen's secretary on the telephone and told her he had a friend with a script that he wanted her boss to read.

"Send it in," the secretary said.

"No way," countered Larry. "I know how that works. I want your boss to have dinner with my friend, and then he can have the script."

"That won't be possible," the secretary said.

Larry persisted. "Ask your boss if he knows anything about Chuck Norris, the World Karate Champion."

The secretary buzzed Allen, who acknowledged that he had heard of me. He arranged to meet me for dinner the following evening at an Italian restaurant in Torrance.

That night I lay in bed pondering the question Allen was certain to ask: "Why will this movie make money?" I have always trusted my subconscious mind and have discovered that if I think about a problem before going to sleep, I often awaken with the answer. At about 2:00 A.M. I awoke from a sound sleep with the perfect reponse to the question.

Dianne went to the dinner with me. It turned out that Allen looked even younger than he was. But he was very down-to-earth, and we all hit it off immediately. With his partner, Michael Leone, he had already produced two successful low-budget films, *Acapulco Gold*, with Marjoe Gortner, and *The Great Smoky Roadblock*, with Henry Fonda. His enthusiasm for me as star of a film convinced me that he would be perfect for my project.

After dinner, Allen stopped by my house to pick up the

script. Before saying goodnight he asked me why I thought this movie would have an audience and make money.

This time I had my response ready. "There are four million karate students in America," I said. "Even though not many other people know who I am, they do. Since I don't fight anymore, the only way they can see me perform is on the screen. If only half of them see the film, that guarantees you a six-million-dollar gross on a million-dollar investment."

"Makes sense to me," Allen said and left with the script. It was 1:00 A.M.

Four hours later Allen awakened me to say that he liked the story and wanted me to star in the film.

Despite his enthusiasm, Allen found it difficult to convince Michael Leone, who raised the money for their films, to get his investors to put up money for a picture that would star an athlete and not an experienced actor. When he told me this I suggested that the next time he and Michael got their investors together he let me talk to them.

Soon after that conversation, Allen called to say that a group of investors was having a screening of a film he and Michael had packaged. Dianne and I flew to Carmel, California, the next night on a private jet that belonged to one of the investors. It was the first time we had ever flown in a private plane. Although it was only a half-hour flight, I very quickly became accustomed to the luxury. It may not be the only way to fly, but it sure was great.

We arrived just after the screening. I was introduced and led to the center of the room. After three years of practice, my level of confidence had grown, and I was comfortable with my presentation. I gave the men a synopsis of the story and told them something about my background in karate and my belief that kids would accept me as a role model. Someone asked the inevitable question: why did I think the picture would make money? By this time my answer was well rehearsed. As I spoke I could sense them calculating the number of karate people who might go see me in a film.

Afterward, I walked around the room and talked with the individual investors. Although they all appeared to be hardheaded businessmen from various walks of life, they seemed more interested in my karate career than in the script. I was on safe ground there and comfortable with my responses.

A couple of days later Michael Leone called to say that his investors were willing to put up a million dollars to do the film. They had agreed to pay me $40,000 to star in it, and he said if it was successful they would consider making two more films with me. After I hung up the phone and relayed the news to Dianne, we danced around our living room together. In 1977, I was flat broke, and $40,000 seemed like all the money in the world to us.

I was so excited that I called Larry Morales to share the news with him.

"You're kidding," he said.

"I swear, it's true."

"If you get two more movies, you'll be set for life," he said.

*   *   *

Ted Post, who had directed Clint Eastwood in *Magnum Force*, was signed to direct *Good Guys Wear Black*, which meant that I would be in good professional hands. Ted decided that since I wasn't an experienced actor I should be surrounded by professionals: James Franciscus, Dana Andrews, Jim Backus, Lloyd Haynes, and Anne Archer. I was delighted to have such a good support system.

They also hired a voice and drama coach for me named Jonathan Harris, a very proper man who enunciated every word as though he were reciting Shakespeare. Jonathan worked with me eight hours a day for three weeks. However, he spent more time teaching me how to speak than helping me recite the dialogue that was actually in the script.

One day he came over to me, put his fingers in my mouth, and stretched it wide open. "Open your mouth, open your mouth," he screamed.

"Jonathan, you're the only man in the world who could do that to me and get away with it," I said when he finally let go.

"I know," he said, and smiled.

Even though I didn't enunciate the way Jonathan wanted, I had learned all the dialogue in the screenplay except for one eight-page block that called for me to debate the merits of the Vietnam War with James Franciscus. The shooting schedule called for this scene to take four days of filming. It was a very difficult scene for me to do because I had to sit through all of it, not moving.

I asked Jonathan to talk to the director and make certain that the scene was filmed toward the end of the schedule so I would have a chance to get into my character. Jonathan said he would take care of it.

As fate would have it, James Franciscus had signed to do another film and would be with us for only four days. One of his key scenes was that humongous one with me. The director decided to film it on the first day of shooting and scheduled it to be shot in one day instead of four.

I had my lines memorized, but on the night before shooting I was so nervous that I had to use every trick I knew to get to sleep.

When we started filming that key scene, I discovered to my horror that Jim had rewritten his lines in the script. I had memorized my speech and the cues that led into it. When he started saying things that weren't in the script I had a terrible time trying to splice in my replies. Worse, I realized that his character's argument was making sense, and that I was not winning the debate as I was supposed to.

To add to my difficulties, the producers invited a reporter to interview me during the lunch hour. The reporter wrote that I was apprehensive and nervous on the first day of shooting. He was dead right.

We started filming at 7:00 A.M. and finished at 4:00 A.M. the following morning. Twenty hours of straight shooting on my first day before the cameras! I felt as though someone had thrown me into the ocean with chains on my feet and told me to swim ashore. It was a horrendous experience, but I reasoned that if I could survive this first scene I could survive the film.

I was insecure at the beginning of the film, but I knew that negative thinking would be destructive. Negative attitudes bring negative emotions, just as positive attitudes encourage positive emotions. I said to myself, I'm going to do the very best I am capable of doing and not worry about the difference in experience between the others and me. And that is what I did.

In the middle of filming *Good Guys Wear Black* I went through the worst emotional experience of my life aside from my brother's death. Earlier in the week, Dianne had gone to the doctor for a routine checkup. One morning as I was leaving for the location she called the doctor. As she was talking to him I saw the color drain from her face. I grabbed the phone and asked the doctor what was wrong. He told me that her Pap smear had come up irregular and he wanted her to have more tests. The tests were positive. Dianne had cancer of the cervix. A hysterectomy was required. Two days later I took Dianne to the hospital and stayed overnight in her room. On the day of surgery, I was with her almost every minute.

That was the roughest day of my life. My mind was constantly on my wife, who also was my best friend. *Cancer* is such a horrible word, and the thought that I might lose her terrified me. Wieland's death had been a terrible experience, but the circumstances surrounding it were uncontrollable. There was nothing I could do to bring him back. Dianne's fate rested in the hands of her doctors. I felt absolutely helpless. I prayed that she would recover. My prayers were answered: the operation was successful, and I was soon able to bring Dianne home.

When the film was finished, everyone congratulated me on doing a commendable job. When I look back on that picture now, I realize that they were just being nice because I was not very good. The first time I saw the picture, I didn't think it was too bad. After the fourth time, however, I considered it the worst movie I had ever seen in my life. But it was the best I could do at the time. The movie was successful despite my lack of experience because I believe I created an image people enjoyed seeing.

It was with a great deal of trepidation that I invited Steve to attend a screening and to give me his reaction. Afterward we had dinner together. "It's not too bad," he said. "But let me give you some advice. You are verbalizing things on the screen that we have already seen. Movies are visual, so don't reiterate something verbally that we have seen visually.

"Next time, let the other actors fill in the plot. When there's something important to say, you be the one to say it. Believe me, audiences will remember what you said. But if you just talk for the sake of talking, they won't remember anything."

He gave me an example of what he meant. In *Bullitt* Steve had a scene with Robert Vaughn in which he was to reply to Vaughn with a long speech. Steve read the speech and realized that it was too wordy. He approached the director, who asked him what he would like to say. Steve crossed out the long speech and wrote one line: "You work your side of the street, and I'll work mine."

"Everyone remembered that line," Steve said. "That's what you have to do in your movies. Read your scripts carefully, and if you don't like some of your lines go over them with the director. Try to convince him to let you say as little as possible and make your lines memorable." (A recent example of this is Clint Eastwood's "Go ahead, make my day." Everyone remembered that line; a song was written about it, and President Reagan even included it in a speech.)

"Put as much of yourself into the character as possible and make it as real as you can," Steve said. "We all have multiple personalities, and you have to draw on them, the light or humorous side as well as the dark and aggressive side. By using those facets of your personality, your character will become more real to you and the audience. Always remember that the real star is someone the audience identifies with."

Despite their enthusiasm for *Good Guys Wear Black*, the producers had problems finding a distributor—none of the distributors had faith in the film's box-office potential. In desperation, the producers decided to distribute the film themselves. They borrowed money, rented theaters for a flat fee for a week or so in small towns, and kept the box-office receipts.

I followed the openings of *Good Guys Wear Black,* from small town to small town. I did interviews at the local schools, with the newspapers, on television, and with anyone who would talk with me. After a few weeks on the road doing ten or twelve interviews a day I had learned to recount the plot of the film in anything from thirty seconds to three minutes, depending on how much time I was allowed. I did one local television show in a small town and gave the condensed version of the plot, after which the interviewer said, "I can't believe you got that much into thirty seconds." I considered that a real compliment.

When I did a television show I always tried to plant the first question with the interviewer. That gave me something to cling to because I'd have the answer right in my head. In that sense, my first acting lines were my own creation. I'd write them in my head before going on. Even if the show's host forgot to ask the question, I was so glued to my prepared answer that I'd blurt it out anyway. It was sort of a comedy of errors, but it got me used to being a public person and having that camera eye staring at me.

Allen Bodoh and Michael Leone began looking for another screenplay for me. I asked Pat Johnson, a close friend who is a writer as well as my senior instructor, to write a script for me. "Since you're a karate champion, let's write a story about a karate fighter," he said.

The screenplay he wrote, entitled *A Force of One,* was about a karate champion named Matt Logan who is convinced by a pretty narcotics officer (played by Jennifer O'Neill) to head up a squad investigating a drug epidemic that is taking over a city. The investigation mysteriously begins to go haywire. One by one the squad members are eliminated by an assassin who is obviously a trained martial artist. To make matters worse, a big martial-arts tournament being held there means that the town is bursting with men who are suspects. At the same time, Logan is training to defend his title against Jerry Sparks (played by Bill Wallace). Logan's adopted son is killed by the drug ring. Only when he gets into the ring in the film's final sequence does Logan realize that Sparks is the unknown assassin and that more than his title is at stake: he must fight for his life.

The climactic fight was filmed in a sports arena in San Diego. There were a lot of extras, including about thirty tough-looking Chicanos. While Bill and I were fighting, they kept throwing things into the ring, causing us to blow scene after scene. No one wanted to say anything to them because they were spoiling for trouble. Of course, we could have called the police, but that might have caused a real hassle. I thought about it and decided that what the gang really wanted was attention. It was only a hunch, but I thought it was worth playing out.

I suggested to the director that we stop filming while I went and talked with them. I sat down in the middle of the group and noticed that some of them had guns and knives. That made me nervous, but I kidded around and asked questions that showed I was interested in them. Finally we struck up a rapport. Some of them had seen *Return of the Dragon*, and they asked me about Bruce and our fight scene in the Colosseum. I responded patiently and fully while the director looked on, biting his fingernails.

Finally they asked if I wanted them to put on a real rumble for the film. I thanked them and said that wouldn't be necessary, but that I would appreciate it if they wouldn't throw things into the ring. They agreed not to.

Had I or anyone else gone down there with a hostile attitude we would have had our hands full. This was another example of the fact that a hostile attitude provokes a hostile response. Because I reacted to them in a friendly manner, they responded similarly.

After *A Force of One* was completed, the producers again had difficulty finding a distribution company. They decided to do exactly what they had done with *Good Guys Wear Black*. So I started all over again on the same trail. I had made some friends on my first trek, so it wasn't quite as stressful the second time around, and the media was a little more responsive to me. But I was on a treadmill. *Good Guys Wear Black* was still showing in various cities, so I would fly to one of them and promote it and then fly to another to promote *A Force of One*. There were times when I arrived in a city and had to think, Now, which movie am I promoting? I stayed on the road nine months with both pictures.

A Force of One grossed more than twenty million dollars, and *Good Guys Wear Black* grossed more than eighteen million, far exceeding any predictions. The producers of my films prospered, as did I. My salary increased from $40,000 to $125,000 to $250,000 per film. When we did *A Force of One,* the producers had a small office with only one secretary. The staff grew to fifty within two years. By the time we made a third film, *The Octagon,* they had a staff of a hundred and had become one of the leading independent studios in Hollywood. My three films alone finally grossed more than a hundred million dollars! American Cinema was able to go public with working capital of sixty million dollars. I was proud to be part of their growth.

The producers then told me that they did not want to do any more Chuck Norris films. Some executives argued with them about letting me go. They were fired. Ironically, the company followed up with three very large-budget films that all bombed at the box office. Very soon after that American Cinema experienced financial difficulties.

Many critics panned my acting in those early films; this really pained me because I had done the best I could. I told Steve that I couldn't understand the critics. "I'm not trying to be an actor like Dustin Hoffman," I said. "I'm just trying to make a film people will enjoy."

Steve laughed. "Look," he said, "the bottom line is that if your movies make money you will continue to make movies. If you get the best reviews in the world but your films bomb at the box office, you'll be unemployed. The only thing you have to worry about is the public. Do they like your movies? If they do, you'll have a long career.''

Steve McQueen died several years later, in 1980. I hadn't seen him for a long time. The pressures of my own work had precluded my teaching him and Chad, so Pat Johnson had taken over as their instructor. When I heard that Steve was dying of cancer I was saddened and tried to contact him. By then, however, he didn't want any of his old friends to see him. He wanted to be remembered as he had been: strong and healthy. Pat, one of the few people Steve allowed to visit him, told me that Steve was optimistic until the very end, determined to beat the cancer that was ravaging his body. That's the kind of guy Steve was; he never gave up on anything.

To this day, I have never forgotten his encouragement and advice.

A man's life is built not on the years he has lived but on the accomplishments he has achieved.

EIGHT

I BELIEVE THAT life is like a large pie, with pieces representing different priorities. My family has always been the biggest portion of my pie, with my profession, training, friends, and outside passions sharing the remainder. Having grown up without a strong father image in a home where there was discord rather than harmony, I wanted my two sons to know that I was there, that I cared, and that I was always in their corner. I am very close to my sons. I have played with them, listened to their problems, held them in my arms when they were hurt, and shared most of the major events, crises, and successes of their lives. One of my biggest gratifications today is that my grown-up sons aren't embarrassed to kiss me hello or goodbye in front of anyone and that they come willingly to me for advice or help if they have problems.

And neither they nor I have ever been ashamed to say, "I love you," three simple words that mean so much and are so rarely said between parents and their children. I never told my father that, and to this day it bothers me that he died alone, not knowing that I loved him despite his faults.

I was determined to give my sons support and love because children growing up in a happy family relationship are better prepared to face the pressures of everyday life. I believe there is too much permissiveness in today's society. Parents are afraid to discipline children for fear that they will grow up with an inferiority complex or resent them. An undisciplined child will usually find it difficult to handle discipline as an adult. Therefore, when an undisciplined child grows up he is likely to become bored or disenchanted with life—he hasn't developed the ability to deal with everyday trials and tribulations. I feel that the main thing parents should do is give their children responsibility.

I tried to instill a strong self-image in my boys while they were growing up and to motivate them to become success-oriented. I wanted them to begin to set goals while they were still in school. And I wanted them to think of themselves as leaders rather than followers: they never had to do something they felt in their heart was wrong just because others were doing it.

I didn't wish for either of my sons to follow in my footsteps. But to help them develop the inner security to handle peer pressures, I had each boy start studying karate when he turned five. I wanted them to study for at least two or three years, in order to gain enough physical proficiency and mental confidence to be able to handle themselves if the need ever arose. I also hoped that through karate training they would learn discipline and gain a sense of commitment.

Mike, the elder, took to karate with enthusiasm. When I realized that he was serious about his training, I put him in a class with Aaron as his instructor. He became so proficient that he won seventeen tournaments in the Pee Wee Division (for children under the age of nine), including the Pee Wee World Championship. When he was about ten years old, however, he asked me if he could give up karate in order to play soccer, baseball, and football. I encouraged him because I wanted him to be his own person and I felt that after five years of karate training he had developed enough inner strength and confidence in himself to be able to handle peer pressure.

Eric also studied with Aaron for three years, but he too preferred American sports, in which he excelled. This was fine with me. His karate training did prove useful, however. When Eric was in the seventh grade he ran afoul of an eighth-grader who was a bully as well as the school drug pusher. Many kids bought from him out of fear. He tried to force Eric to take a marijuana cigarette from him, and they got into a fight. Eric worked him over and forced him to eat the marijuana cigarette. The school principal called me in to his office.

"I'm going to discipline Eric for fighting," he told me.

"No, you're not," I retorted. "Whenever anybody tries to give one of them drugs, my boys have my permission to refuse any way they want to." That ended the matter.

While my sons were still in school I tried to participate in their outside activities. There was a basketball hoop in our back yard, and we played two-on-one for hours. I coached them in Little League baseball for years and was always at their games. I didn't want their friends to think of me only as an actor, so I'd have them come over to the house, where we'd barbecue hamburgers. After they saw me often enough, the glamour of my being a film star wore off. Their friends soon began to know me as a person and think of me only as Mike and Eric's dad.

My sons loved football and made their high school teams, which made me very proud. I usually refused to work during the season because I wanted to be present at their games. In 1981 I was offered a starring role in *Forced Vengeance*, which was to be filmed in Hong Kong. I was going to turn it down because it was scheduled to be made during the football season and Eric was on his high school team. I didn't want to miss any of his games.

When I discussed my decision with the family, Eric said, "I'm only a junior, Dad, so I'll probably be sitting on the bench most of the time. Why don't you do the movie and try to be home next year when I'm a senior?"

I thought it over and decided that as long as Eric was certain that he was going to sit on the bench and not play I might as well go to Hong Kong to make the picture. I phoned home every other day to talk with the family.

Instead of sitting on the bench, however, Eric made first-string offense *and* defense.

When I returned home from Hong Kong I learned that Eric had made second-string California Interscholastic Federation. This news filled me with pride, but I was miserable that I had missed his games.

After I made *Lone Wolf McQuade* in 1982 I decided to take the next year off because it was Eric's last year in high school. I told Dianne, "Eric is our last child, and I am going to stay home and see his games." I was gratified that I did because he had a good year and I was there to share it with him.

When Mike was fifteen he told me that he wanted to be an actor. It happened that I had just been offered a film, *The Octagon*. There was a perfect role in it for him: he could play me as a young boy. Mike tested for the role and got it.

Mike took to acting after *The Octagon* and decided to pursue it as a career. His first feature, *Born American*, a story of three college students hiking in Finland who mistakenly cross the border into Russia, was recently released.

Dianne and I are very family-oriented as well as child-oriented; many of our relatives live in the Orange County area. Our house is very secluded and remote, and none of our neighbors are involved with the film business. We seldom go to Hollywood parties, and whenever possible we spend time with family. As a result, our kids have grown up with a good family support system. I feel that this is extremely important for anyone, but especially for youngsters.

*   *   *

I try to include my family in everything I do. My passion now is off-road racing, which I have been involved in for the past six years. Until I did it myself, I always wondered what there was about racing that enticed so many stars, including James Dean, Steve McQueen, Paul Newman, James Garner, and a host of others. Now I understand their ardor. I have found few things more exciting and challenging than pushing a vehicle and myself to the outer limits of our capabilities. And I find racing to be a good form of relaxation because when I am driving my mind is totally focused. I am completely centered. When the race is over, I relax thoroughly from exhaustion.

I entered my first race in 1981, driving a souped-up Nissan truck in the Frontier 100 Mile Off-Road Race and competing against celebrity drivers who had been racing for years. I placed first. The other drivers couldn't understand how a novice could beat them all. The reason was that I was in very good physical shape, which meant that I could take the pounding and that my concentration was intense. I won again in 1982 and 1983.

In 1984 I entered a 250-mile celebrity off-road race in Nevada with Eric, then nineteen years old, as my codriver. I told Eric I would drive the first 125 miles and he could drive the second half. There were eight trucks in the race, leaving the starting line at one-minute intervals; we were six minutes behind the lead vehicle. In short order we passed the truck that had left just before us. Two journalists were in the next truck, driving cautiously, as though they were on a Sunday outing. They pulled over to let us pass and waved us on. We continued passing trucks until, in the distance, I saw the trail of dust from the leader.

I put the pedal to the metal but missed a turn. We went into a slide and began to roll over. As the truck thumped over, Eric asked, "Dad, are you OK?"

"I'm fine," I said. "How about you?"

After three full rollovers in the desert we came to rest on Eric's side of the truck. Someone came running up, shouting, "Gas is leaking!"

I undid my safety straps, grabbed Eric, and pulled him out of the cab. We discovered only a small leak in the gas tank, but the windshield was broken out. "Maybe it will still run," Eric said.

We pushed the truck back up onto its wheels. It started. Just as we were taking off, the two journalists we had passed earlier rolled up and stopped to ask whether we were OK. Assured that we were fine, they took off.

A few minutes later, we overtook them and they waved. Eight miles before the midway point of the race, we got a flat tire. While we were changing it, the journalists went by again. Minutes later we again shot by them, but just before the halfway point we had to make a pit stop. The journalists waved as they passed.

It took the crew half an hour to get us going. With Eric at the wheel, we passed the journalists once more. About forty miles from the finish line, we lost the entire front end of the truck. That was the end of the race for us, but not for the journalists. They passed us again and wound up taking second place.

In 1985 Eric and I entered another race, which my brother Aaron and his codriver, Brock Glover, won. Eric and I came in a close second.

In 1986 Aaron and I drove together in a 400-mile desert race against professionals. We started off in seventh place and made it to second before we got sand in the fuel lines and had to drop out of the running.

My biggest problem with Aaron, who is twelve years younger than me, was the fact that as he got older I kept treating him like a son because I always remembered how, when Mom was working, I had baby-sat for and taken care of him. I finally had to realize that he wasn't a son or a kid brother any longer: he was a man in his twenties, and I had to stop treating him like a boy.

I had the same problem with my sons, who are now twenty-two and twenty-five. Until quite recently, I still thought of them as kids, although they are men and adults. But I am still concerned about them, and I think they like that.

For me, friendship is like marriage. It's as hard to find a close friend as it is to find a good spouse, and when you do find one you want to hang on. You find weaknesses and strengths in your friends, things that drive you crazy and things that make you happy. But you take them all on balance and allow for the good as well as the bad. Many times I've seen people with friends who have done nothing but good for them over the years. Then that friend does one bad thing, and the friendship ends because the only thing remembered is the bad, not the good.

I have found that when you have an enthusiasm about life, you attract people with the same passion. My close friends have the same positive spirit about life that I have. They, too, value friendship. They can be counted on. Like me, they believe that the only thing you can give and still keep in life is your word. Most of them were close to me before I went into the movie business. I knew them when they were as dirt-poor as I was, and I believe I've retained those friendships because when I started making movies I was in my mid-thirties and they had long since proved themselves. The quality I cherish about these men is that they are positive and motivated.

The four men whom I would bet my life on and who have been closest to me for decades are successful in their own careers. Bob Wall was my contemporary in karate competitions, a world champion, himself and, later, my business partner. He now has a flourishing real-estate business.

I met Pat Johnson in 1967 at a tournament in Cleveland, Ohio, when I fought Skipper Mullins and won the Grand Championship. Pat was one of the contestants; I liked him and told him that I hoped he would call me if he ever got to Los Angeles. Two months later, he called from the bus station and I went to pick him up. Pat lived with Dianne and me for a few months and then I put him in charge of the Sherman Oaks school. Pat is a unique person, a born leader. He is also one of the best karate instructors in the business. He took over a school that had been failing and turned it into one of the most profitable schools in Los

Angeles. Pat is now doing well as a stunt coordinator in the film business and has written the screenplays for two of my pictures.

Something as casual as a meeting with a stranger can often change the course of one's life. A seemingly insignificant meeting may eventually wind up as one of the most important events in your life. I first met Larry Morales twenty-four years ago in a line for an airplane to San Francisco. He was traveling with one of my students, who introduced us. My student asked if I wanted to sit with them on the plane. I wasn't certain whether to read or go join them; finally I decided to join them. Larry was outgoing, funny, and positive-thinking. By the time we got to San Francisco, we were friends. Larry became my neighbor and confidant and now has a thriving machine-shop business.

It was Larry who called up Allen Bodoh for me and made the contact that got me started in the film business. I often wonder: if I had never met Larry, would I be an actor today?

My newest close friend is Mike Emery, who has a prosperous law practice. Mike and I met soon after I completed *Good Guys Wear Black*. At that time no one was interested in me as an actor, and I was studying with drama coach Zena Provendie. Zena convinced Mike, who had represented many top stars over the years, to see me. At the time, he was developing his law practice and was not interested in handling any more stars, much less an unknown. But he saw the film and took me on. For the last decade, Mike has negotiated all my contracts and handled my career and finances, shrewdly conserving and investing my money so that I need not concern myself about financial security for the rest of my life.

It takes a long time for someone to push me to the point of terminating a friendship, because I always think of the good times shared rather than the bad.

When I work on a film I like to be surrounded by people I like, respect, and trust. As a result, my films are generally made with compatible people. Aaron, who has been a stunt coordinator on many films, including mine, is now a director. In 1987 he directed *Braddock: Missing in Action III;* my sons have worked in various capacities with me; my brother-in-law, Mark Holochek, acted in *Breaker! Breaker!* as a villain. Many of my black belts work as stuntmen or actors.

Howard Jackson, who was the World Karate Association Welterweight World Champion, has appeared in my films and is now my workout partner and travels with me. Bob Wall has had roles in many of my films. Bill "Superfoot" Wallace, who won the World Middleweight title the year I retired undefeated and who himself retired undefeated in 1982, was my nemesis in *A Force of One*. I met Richard Norton, one of the top weapons experts in the world, in Australia, and he played my nemesis in *The Octagon*. He is now starring in his own films.

Frequently, when young people become successful in the movie business and get a certain amount of popularity, their values and attitudes change. They haven't yet had

173

time to mature to the point where they can deal with success.

I think that is probably due to deep-seated insecurities and the same paranoia that plagued Steve McQueen. When he became successful, Steve believed that everyone wanted something from him. In my case, my friends had stuck with me through the bad times, so I had no reason to be suspicious of them when things were going well.

I cherish my friends. They, along with my family, are an integral part of my personal support system. Were it not for that support system, I would not be a happy man today, nor would I have been able to achieve success.

Think of yourself as a leader rather than a follower. Your subconscious mind will take it as a fact, and you will act accordingly.

Never be ashamed to say "I love you." Those three words that mean so much are not said often enough.

NINE

ACTING WAS A REAL challenge for me because it was so
different from karate. In karate competition you are never
to reveal anger or fear to your opponent. For years I taught
myself to control my emotions and not to show them.
When I began to act, I suddenly had to learn to bring all
those guarded feelings to the surface. I tried to find a
similarity between the two professions and realized that the
essence of a dramatic scene is usually conflict—and conflict is the substance of tournament karate.

Before each tournament I used to rehearse the fight in
my mind. I find it's much the same with acting. I visualize
a scene beforehand, and if I have the right attitude, I am
successful in executing it. I don't worry about the words, I
just want to get the feeling out. Intelligence, instinct, and

technique are, in my view, key ingredients of a good actor, just as they are important factors in the making of a karate champion.

I enjoy playing strong roles, but it's essential that the part make either physical or emotional demands on me. I am well aware that, whatever my role, kids believe it's Chuck Norris up there on the screen, and not whatever character I am playing. Therefore I won't do anything in my movies that's detrimental to that image. If I were to smoke dope or snort cocaine they might say, "Well, Chuck does it, so it must be OK." And I won't play heavy-duty sex scenes. As far as I am concerned, sex scenes harm youngsters, who are not able to release the sexual tension those scenes build. But when they watch a fight scene, they can start yelling and getting into the action. That's tension they can safely release. As long as I am perceived as a role model, I intend to be a positive one who projects an image kids can relate to and emulate. Kids know that, and so do their parents.

I try to put as much of myself as possible into the characters I play. As an actor who is a former martial-arts champion and instructor, I try to promote the philosophical concepts of the arts so youngsters will appreciate that there's more to karate than fighting. I never exploit my ability to fight because there is a difference between action and violence. The characters I play use their skills only as a last resort. (There has always been violence on the screen, and certain groups claim that some antisocial behavior can be traced to these violent films. I believe that's hogwash. The violence on the television news programs is much more harmful because it's real. We all have the potential to be violent, but we have to learn to control those impulses.)

The common theme of the movies I choose to do is this: you must strive to be the best you can be, regardless of what you pursue. We've all had obstacles to overcome in our lives, whether we're young or old. I like my movies to be about a plausible person doing implausible things, facing apparently insurmountable obstacles and successfully dealing with them.

Most of my films are modern-day versions of the old cowboy movies I grew up watching. In those movies as well as in mine, the good guy always wins. There's always somebody for the audience to cheer, somebody for them to identify with.

The Octagon, my eighth film, was the story of a young man named Scott James who is raised by a martial-arts master in a wild area of Japan. His foster-brother is a Japanese boy named Seikura. The boys grow up together and are taught all the master's fighting secrets. When the boys come of age, Seikura, in a burst of egoism, turns out to be a bad loser. He is dismissed by the old master, who warns Scott that Seikura will now be his lifelong enemy. My son Mike played me as a young boy in the flashback scenes.

Years later, Scott (my character) becomes romantically involved with a young ballerina. In a terrorist attack, the ballerina and her family are slaughtered, apparently by Ninjas, a legendary sect of black-garbed Japanese assassins active during that country's feudal period. Scott knows intellectually that the sect no longer exists as such, but he has seen and fought with what certainly appear to be Ninjas. He is convinced that only Seikura could be behind these killers.

The climax of the film is a sword fight in the midst of a blazing inferno. The story was somewhat convoluted, but the action was nonstop. The movie received good notices. *New York* magazine reported that I "was certainly impressive in action" and added that "Movies like *The Octagon* glory in something genuine—a love of fighting and a love of prowess, two qualities dependably popular the world over. If international mass culture has a bedrock, this is it."

Making a good action film is a combination of some of the toughest elements of both acting and athletics. I doubt that many people realize how complex it is to go through a series of moves, say lines with your head turned at the correct angle, and end up on the spot where the director wants you.

Since I have so many elements to consider, there's no way I can do justice to choreographing my own films. This is where Aaron takes over. We collaborate on all the action sequences, and then he sets them up and hires the stuntmen. In every action scene we try to establish a realistic base. This is in contrast to the Hong Kong kung-fu

movies in which the fight scenes are too obviously prear-
ranged: kicks and punches are done by the numbers and
without a lot of power. In those films, kicks miss by
around a foot, but with the camera angle and added sound
they appear to be direct hits.

I always work with my own stuntmen because they
know my timing. If they don't move at exactly the right
instant, they'll get clipped. Audiences today are familiar
with camera angles, so I work on getting my kicks so
close—within a fraction of an inch—that even with the
camera at a side angle the audience can't see the near miss
required to protect the actors.

Occasionally, when we use actors who are not stuntmen,
they get hurt accidentally, just as the professionals do.
This happened while I was making *The Octagon*, when I
was just beginning to feel confident as an actor but was
still slugging my way through roles.

One of the big fight scenes in the film took place inside
a walled-in enclosure that was the headquarters of the
Ninjas. We started filming at 6:00 P.M. and ten hours later
were still in the heat of battle. Finally there was just one
fight sequence left. But it was 4:00 A. M., and everyone
was exhausted. The director told Aaron that we would
finish the scene the next day. Aaron sent home the four
stuntmen I had not yet fought. Five minutes later the
director changed his mind and announced, "Let's do this
last scene before it gets light." Aaron protested that the
stuntmen had left, but the director told him to figure
something out.

There were still two stuntmen on the set, John Barrett and Jay DePland, and Aaron made three, but we were one man shy. At this point a well-built young film technician approached Aaron and said he would like to be a stunt-man. Aaron asked whether he had ever done any stunt work before. The young man admitted that he didn't have any experience. "This may be a little tougher than you think," Aaron said. "Chuck makes a little contact when he hits."

"That's OK with me," said the young man. "I'm in good shape. Don't worry about it."

Since the director was determined to shoot the sequence, Aaron had no choice. He dressed the young volunteer in Ninja clothes and laid out the scene in which I was to walk into a maze and be attacked by four Ninjas. The newcomer was to attempt to grab me from behind. I would back-kick him in the stomach and he would go down. After a re-hearsal I told Aaron to put a chest-pad under the young man's shirt so I wouldn't have to worry about hurting him. But the technician refused, saying, "The others aren't wearing pads, so I'm not going to."

We took our places. The cameras started rolling. The director called "Action." When the young man attacked, I kicked him, making light contact. His eyes rolled back into his head, and he dropped instantly. I looked down, saw him convulsing on the ground, and thought, Oh, my God, I've hurt him.

But the cameras were still rolling, and the scene called for John Barrett to attack me from behind. My stuntmen know that in order to make a fight look real they have to attack me aggressively. John charged me and I turned to face him, but my mind was a total blank: I had forgotten what I was supposed to do. I shifted sideways and punched John in the side of the head, actually knocking him out. Aaron, who was the third man to attack, heard the contact but jumped out at me anyway. I spun instinctively and kicked him in the head, knocking him out too. Jay, who was supposed to be next, looked down at the inert bodies and shouted, "I'm not coming down there!" Fortunately everyone recovered, and the scene was redone, but I put a big pad on the young man's stomach.

For another scene in *The Octagon* I had to fight several Ninjas who came out of the water to assault me while I was standing on a platform. Since the Ninjas wore masks, I could use the same stuntmen in several fight scenes. I let John Barrett climb onto the platform and attempt to stab me. At that point, I was to jump up and do a cartwheel in the air, hitting John in the chest with my heels. John was to drop down with his head hanging over the side of the platform while I put my foot on his chin and pushed his head under the water. He was supposed to struggle for a few beats. When he "died" I was to let up. That was the plan, but this was not John's night.

Before the scene started I told John to take a deep breath so that when he struggled underwater he would have enough air in his lungs. As luck would have it, the air outside was damp and cold. When we started the scene John took a breath, but the Ninja mask clung to his face, keeping the air out of his lungs. John went over the side as planned and began struggling. He's sure fighting harder now than he did in the rehearsal, I thought, not realizing that he was panicked and really fighting for air. I estimated that he could hold his breath for quite a while, so I kept holding him under the water. Finally John stopped struggling. I didn't know it, but he was starting to pass out. When I took my foot off his face John flew out of the water, gasping for breath. He had not been faking.

The following year, 1980, I made *An Eye for an Eye*, the story of Sean Kane, a San Francisco narcotics cop whose partner is ambushed and burned to death in the opening sequences. Kane pursues the gunmen and corners one, sending him flying through the window of a high-rise building and onto the roof of a car. Kane speculates that he and his partner have been set up. After being reprimanded by his captain for excessive violence, Kane hands in his gun and badge. He settles down to a peaceful life with his Chinese girlfriend, Linda Chan, daughter of his *sensei* (martial-arts teacher). Linda, who is investigating drug smuggling in the San Francisco area, is terrorized at a BART (Bay Area Rapid Transit) station by a giant, played by Professor Toru Tanaka, who was the archetypal Oriental bad guy of Wrestling's Golden Quarter-Century (1945 -1970). Linda escapes long enough to call Kane and tell him that she has the goods on the drug ring. By the time Kane reaches her, though, it's too late. The rest of the film revolves around his revenge.

My brother Aaron played the part of the killer in the opening scene, and when I kicked him out of the four-story window his head accidentally hit the top of the window jamb, gashing his head and knocking him off balance. He was unable to regain his balance during his fall to the pad on the ground. Instead of falling on his back, he landed on his side and banged his knees together, breaking one of his legs. The director wanted to rush him to the hospital, but Aaron refused to go until the shot of him lying on top of the car was taken. Aaron finished choreographing the film with a cast on his leg.

The Washington Post didn't like the movie and said that I looked like "Hans Brinker, grown up to be a palooka, because of that little Dutch-boy haircut that crowns his thick, long-jawed, mournful mug." The *New York Times* said that the fight scenes looked "phony," and *People* called the film "insidious Hollywood poppycock." *Variety*, however, said that "Norris's acting is improving and his balletic fighting and kicking skills remain tops in the field. He is the current champ of the chop-socky genre."

I liked the former sentence but I could have done without the latter. I didn't think my films were in the Hong Kong chop-socky mode.

Despite the mixed reviews, I was signed by Columbia Studios to make a picture entitled *Silent Rage*. It was based on a story by Aaron, who felt it was time I played a lover as well as a fighter. Aaron also got an associate producer's credit. I played Dan Stevens, a tough lawman in a small town in the American Southwest. The film opens with a brutal murder by a psychotic named John Kirby, who is driven to violence by the shrill voices of children playing. I arrive on the scene, but he is dying from a shotgun blast from one of my deputies. An ambulance takes Kirby to a hospital that is part of a genetic clinic. Kirby expires as the doctors debate. Finally they inject a secret chemical called Mitogen 35 into him. The injection not only brings Kirby back to life but gives him superhuman strength as well as the ability to heal any wound almost immediately. Kirby goes on a rampage, killing everyone he thinks has harmed him or might harm him. My character, Stevens, finally confronts and kills him in a fight to the death.

In one scene of the film there is a fight in which I wipe out an entire gang of bikers. Most of the bikers were not actors but real-life Hell's Angels types. We were filming in a rival gang's territory, so several members of our group stood around with various weapons to protect their comrades. Fortunately the fight scene was completed without incident.

At the end of the film I had to fight the psycho, played by Brian Libby. Brian decided he wanted to do the fight himself rather than be doubled. I agreed because that way we wouldn't have to work around various camera angles. Brian attacked. I spun around, got him in a judo hold, and threw him to the ground. He fell in pain: he had cracked two ribs. Aaron suggested that we bring in a double.

"No," Brian said, "I can handle it." So he was taped up and we continued. In the next sequence I was to do a flying-scissors take-down. I flipped Brian to the ground. This time he sprained his ankle. He was taped up again and we continued the fight. We finished the scene at daybreak, and Brian was rushed to the hospital. He was a gutsy guy.

Silent Rage was my first film with a heavy love scene, which called for me to make love with actress Toni Kalem. It was a mild scene by most standards, but as the *New York Times* reported, "In the scene where Mr. Norris and Ms. Kalem make love, Mr. Norris is shirtless more often than Ms. Kalem, which is probably a first."

In 1982 MGM signed me to do *Forced Vengeance,* the film I intended to turn down because of Eric's football season. Although I didn't much like the script, the studio executives convinced me to do it. I should have gone with my gut feeling because it was one of my least successful pictures.

The script called for my character, Josh Randall, an ex-member of the Special Forces, to take a job as head of security in a casino called The Lucky Dragon. When the owners, who are Randall's friends, refuse to sell out to a local syndicate, all hell breaks loose.

The villain, a paid assassin who rapes and murders Randall's lady, was played by Sakaguchi Sejii, a former All-Japan judo champion and a professional wrestler.

At 6'6" and 286 pounds, Sakaguchi was a formidable opponent.

In one part of the climactic fight scene, I climbed up on a mantel and dove at Sakaguchi, hitting his chest with my shoulder. It was like hitting a solid wall. Later in the fight I was supposed to run and dive at him, hitting him again and knocking him into a bathroom. I did my leap, knocking him off his feet. We crashed through the door together. Somehow or other I wound up underneath him. With his weight, the fall just about killed me. As the fight continued, I was to force Sakaguchi's head into a toilet bowl and try to drown him as he struggled. He was then to break loose, and the filming would stop while the crew loosened the bolts on the commode so he could wrench it up and throw it at me. But Sakaguchi didn't understand the instructions. Before the director could yell, "Cut," Sakaguchi tore the commode, bolts and all, out of the floor, spraying water everywhere. I saw the commode coming, but I thought it was going to hit the floor first and then roll toward me. Sakaguchi was so strong, however, that he was able to throw the heavy bowl directly to the spot where I was lying on the floor. Luckily I rolled out of the way in time. He then picked me up and threw me through a window so hard that I flew over the pads that were placed outside for me to land on and hit the ground instead. The entire scene, fortunately, was on film. But Sakaguchi had given me a good beating.

Filmed in Hong Kong, *Forced Vengeance* was visually

powerful, but it was also the most violent film I had ever made. *People* magazine complained that "the plot is rickety with age." *Variety,* the film trade paper, said that "For Norris, who has given signs of trying to graduate from the chop-socky genre, this is a step backwards."

For a long time I had been mulling over an idea for a film to be entitled *The Last of the Breed,* a sort of contemporary version of the John Wayne Westerns that had so enthralled me as a kid in Oklahoma. Eventually my ideas were translated into a script for a film called *Lone Wolf McQuade.*

When I first read the screenplay, the lead character, Texas Ranger James J. "Lone Wolf" McQuade, was described as a scruffy person with meanness glaring through his eyes and clothes that looked as though they hadn't been washed in weeks. The character was so opposite to how I am in real life that it took me a while before I decided to take the chance and do the role.

The film opens with a bearded McQuade standing on a desert bluff and looking through a rifle scope at some men who are driving horses through winding sandy passages toward some waiting vehicles. On another bluff, a group of police prepares to head them off. The police move in, using a bullhorn to announce that the rustlers are under arrest.

The rustlers laugh and open fire. The outnumbered police are soon flanked and captured. As the police are about to be executed, McQuade raises his rifle and fires a few incendiary rounds into the rustlers' vehicles, blowing them up and throwing the rustlers into confusion.

They realize that a lone man is causing the havoc. One of them taunts, "Hey, you should stand up like a man." McQuade complies and doesn't flinch when a shot is fired at him; he raises his rifle and blows the man away. The leader of the gang puts a gun to a policeman's head and murders him. He then grabs another officer and waits for McQuade's next move.

In a scene reminiscent of many of the Westerns I loved, McQuade comes down off the mountain with the sun at his back to face the men alone. He wipes out the gang in the shoot-out that follows.

MQuade's captain is not impressed with his feat. The captain's notion of a Texas Ranger is a model citizen, a pillar of the community, and a churchgoing man who has a loving wife and kids. Additionally, the local paper has accused McQuade of being a brutal and out-of-date member of the force.

Meanwhile, McQuade's estranged wife plans to move out of the area with their daughter, Sally. Sally and her boyfriend witness the hijacking of an arms shipment. He is killed, and she is left for dead by the side of the road. McQuade breaks up the ring run by Rawley Wilkes (played by David Carradine) and has the obligatory last-scene battle with him.

Lone Wolf McQuade got an "R" rating (meaning that

the film was restricted to adults) because Richard Heffner, head of the Motion Picture Association of America (the organization that rates pictures for audiences), thought the film was too violent. Orion Pictures, the producers, protested because a "PG" (parental guidance) rating was necessary so children could see the film. When the rating board stood pat, Orion flew me to New York to plead our case.

I had debated with Heffner before on *Good Guys Wear Black* and had prevailed. In this, as on the previous occasion, I gave Heffner my philosophy: there are very few movies with positive heroes on the screen, movies in which a man fights only when he has to. "That's what my movies are all about," I said. I referred to the Westerns I had seen as a child, using John Wayne as a prime example of the man who fights back only when cornered. I told Heffner that I had been a karate instructor for twenty years; I had had a strong influence on kids as a teacher and wanted to have that same influence in a positive way as an actor. "I would never do anything detrimental to that image," I said. "You can't take McQuade seriously. He's fun." I won the case on appeal, and the film was released with a "PG" rating.

Lone Wolf McQuade was a transition film for me. Many critics acknowledged that it was a big step forward for me as an actor. Even though there were a few big fight scenes in which I used karate, there was no way it could be called a kung-fu or martial-arts film: it was a simple action-adventure picture. The scruffy, bearded character I played appealed to many people who had no interest in the martial arts.

It did well at the box office. The most gratifying personal reward for me, however, came from a most unexpected source. One day I received a telephone call from the Make A Wish Foundation, an organization dedicated to helping terminally ill children achieve a wish. They said that Michael Majia, a five-year-old boy who was dying of leukemia, wanted to have a photograph of me. Rather than just send a picture, I telephoned his mother and made a date for a visit. When I arrived at the Majia apartment in Bellflower, which is near my home, Michael was out with his father. While waiting for them to get back, I talked with his mother, Debbie, who told me that Michael had had leukemia since he was three years old. While he was confined to his hospital room, he watched *Lone Wolf McQuade* over and over on a video cassette recorder. "I like you a lot," she said kiddingly, "but I'm getting really tired of seeing your movie. I've seen it thirty times!"

Michael finally arrived with his father. He was a frail little boy, almost bald. I evaluate people by looking in their eyes. As I looked into Michael's, I was aware that his treatments had put him through extreme pain. At the same time, I was conscious of a spirit of inner strength such as I had rarely encountered even in an adult. Inner strength is in everyone, but most of the time we have to work hard to bring it out. But it radiated from this rare youngster who had been so severely tested.

When his mother asked Michael whether he recognized me, he shook his head yes and came running at me. He jumped into my lap and wrapped his thin arms around my neck. We talked for almost an hour; mostly about my karate background and how I had gotten started in movies. Then we got on the living-room floor and I taught him some karate moves. But he'd had a chemotherapy treatment that day, so he was obviously exhausted.

I learned that he was taking the ultimate dose of chemotherapy and that it was extremely painful for him. Despite the fact that the treatments made him violently sick, he maintained a very positive attitude.

After that visit, our friendship flourished. He sat on my lap through a private screening of a film I had just completed, even though he was so weak he had to fight to stay alert. Unfortunately I had to leave town to work on a film, but I called Michael in the middle of December to wish him a merry Christmas. I told him I hoped Santa would bring him everything he wished for. He thanked me and said, "I love you very much." I told him that I loved him, too.

When I returned home that summer I called Michael. His mother told me he had died the previous month. Tears came to my eyes and I whispered, more to myself than her, that I wished I could have done more. She told me that I had done everything possible for him. She also said

191

that Michael had told her matter-of-factly that he wanted to stop taking treatments because "God wants me." Before he died, he went back into the hospital. At his request the chemotherapy treatments stopped, and he prepared himself to die. Through it all, he never once complained. Michael died watching *Lone Wolf McQuade*, with my picture in his hands.

As I spoke with his mother, I felt a crushing sadness. I visualized the little boy with his vibrant smile. Michael was a child who appreciated the time he had on earth, a child who never complained about his disease and pain or asked, "Why me?"

The strength of that little boy touched me. Kids that age are usually whining about something, yet this little fellow never complained. In fact, I'd just had a hernia operation and I was still complaining. But Michael died without a whimper.

You can learn about life from the most unexpected sources. This keen little boy taught me something about inner strength, the ability to accept fierce pain without complaint and still keep fighting, the ability to accept the inevitable with grace and style. He was only five years old, and he hadn't had time enough on this earth to experience many things. The fact that he was able to say "God wants me" has to make anyone believe that there *is* a God. Besides teaching me about courage, Michael also reaffirmed for me how fragile our lives really are and how we should appreciate every moment of life that God allows us. Now, when things start getting me down, I remember that smiling little boy who thought life was the greatest experience in the world and who lived every day to its fullest.

One of the keys to inner strength is to accept the inevitable with grace and style.

TEN

EVER SINCE MY brother Wieland's death in Vietnam, I had wanted to do homage to his memory. In 1983, director Lance Hool came to me with a screenplay about American POWs in Vietnam. Films about the Vietnam War were not in vogue then, and I went from one production company to another trying to convince them to make such a film. I was rejected at each meeting, but I was persistent and kept thinking positively. I knew I could make it happen if I persevered.

Finally Lance suggested that Cannon Films might be interested in producing it. The executives there said they already had a screenplay about the rescue of some POWs but they liked our script too. It was decided to film both pictures back-to-back (one after the other).

Even though my character, Colonel James Braddock, is the only one who appears in both films, the two form a pair. The first to be completed and released was *Missing in Action,* the story of Colonel Braddock's postwar return to Vietnam to rescue MIAs. The second to be released was *Missing in Action 2: The Beginning,* the story of Braddock's seven years as an MIA in Vietnam.

Missing in Action was filmed in the Philippines on a difficult as well as hazardous location. There were also some near disasters. During one scene I had to drive along the banks of a river while the Vietcong were shooting at me. To give the impression that bullets were landing all around me, the special-effects man planted squibs (electrical firing devices used to simulate bullet hits) inside the truck. Some of the squibs were too close to my face. When they exploded, powder and debris hit me and took a chunk out of my nose. My eyebrows had to be stitched, and a piece of flesh-colored plastic had to be taped over my nose so we could continue filming.

Another scene I remember vividly called for me to lead four MIAs chest-deep into the ocean, where we were supposed to be rescued by a helicopter. The plan was for the chopper pilot to fly over us and drop a ladder down. I was to hold the ladder while the MIAs climbed into the helicopter. For the end of the scene, a double was to be used. The helicopter would fly off toward the horizon with my double dangling below it.

Unfortunately, a typhoon had just swept through the islands, and the wind was blowing hard. Aaron was nervous about this shot, afraid the stunt double might get blown up into the blades. We decided that I would hold on to the ladder and let the helicopter lift me about a foot out of the water and then lower me. Everything went according to plan. I was up to my neck in the water, an M-16 across my shoulder, when I grabbed the ladder. But instead of hovering for a moment the helicopter continued on up. The next thing I knew I was 300 feet up in the air, clutching the ladder for dear life and looking down. The only thing that entered my mind was, If I let go, will the drop kill me? The pilot flew over the film crew, and I saw them staring up at me agape.

Aaron, who was aware of the pilot's error, panicked and jumped into a boat to chase after me. An assistant director got on the radio and finally contacted the Filipino pilot, who learned that I was still hanging on to the ladder. The pilot swung around immediately and lowered me onto the beach. Later I asked Aaron whether he thought the drop from the helicopter to the water would have killed me. "You'd have been dead as a doornail," he said.

The production also had its funny moments. In one jungle scene I was to fight two Vietcong, played by our stuntmen, one of whom was John Barrett. John's skin color was too fair for him to pass for a Vietnamese, so we had to make him darker. Aaron dug into some mud and started rubbing it all over John's face, eyes, mouth, and chin. John began to sniff and said, "This stuff smells like shit." Aaron put his hand up to his nose, smelled it, said, "It *is* shit," and started gagging. John, who was totally caked with poop, started dashing around madly trying to get it off. He finally dove into the river. I laughed so hard my stomach hurt. Later we learned that the jungle location was near a village, and some sewage had worked its way down to our particular area.

In the climax of the film, I barge into a Saigon hearing room where a conference on American soldiers still trapped in Southeast Asia is reaching the safe, standard conclusion that there are none. With me is a band of prisoners I have just freed from a Vietcong slave camp.

When the film opened, I saw it in a theater in Westwood, California. The biggest thrill of my life came when the audience gave that scene a standing ovation.

MIA took off like a rocket when it was released. It earned more than six million dollars during its first weekend and immediately rose to the number-one position on the charts. It also received some good reviews. But the best praise came from a girl who told me she had taken her dad, a vet, to see the film. "It was the first time I ever saw him cry," she said. *MIA* became the top-grossing independent film of 1984.

Missing in Action 2: The Beginning, is the story of several MIAs who have been held captive for many years in a POW camp run by Colonel Yin, a sadistic Vietnamese who is determined to force Braddock to sign a confession of crimes against the Vietnamese people. Yin tortures Braddock, who refuses to break. When a fellow prisoner is dying of malaria, Braddock agrees to sign a phony confession if Yin will give the man a shot that will save his life.

But Yin gives the man an overdose of heroin instead and then has him dragged into the compound. Gasoline is poured on him and he is burned alive while I am forced to watch. It was one of the most difficult scenes I have ever done as an actor.

The footage of the man burning was shot one day, and my reaction to the event was filmed the next. That meant I really had nothing to react to—I had to draw my emotion from my gut. I told the crew, "This is a one-shot deal," because to pull up that kind of intense feeling would be very difficult. I imagined seeing my brother Wieland when we buried him. That visualization brought up the necessary powerful emotions, but I was emotionally drained.

One of Yin's tortures called for Braddock to be hung by the ankles with a sack over his head, a live rat inside it. When Braddock is brought up, the rat is between his teeth, dead. This turned out to be one of the most unpleasant sequences of my film career.

On the day the scene was to be filmed no one had been able to find a fake rat for me to put in my mouth. "What do you plan to put in the sack?" I asked. Silence. I approached the director, who said that since the prop man hadn't been able to get a fake rat, we were going to have to cheat it somehow. I asked how he planned to do that. After a few moments of thought, he said we would have to cancel the scene. It was an important shot because this torture had in fact been inflicted on MIAs. I suggested that they get a real rat and kill it. As they wrapped the sack over my head I put the rat in my mouth. Then I was hung upside down with phony blood seeping into my mouth.

That- night, Dianne, who usually visits me for a few weeks on locations, took my toothbrush and put it on the other side of the sink from hers. She refused to kiss me for almost a week.

Both films were my tribute to Wieland. They also served as a statement on behalf of the families of the nearly 2,500 soldiers still unaccounted for in Southeast Asia. My heart goes out to those families because even though losing Wieland was a tragic experience for me, at least I know that he is dead and where he is buried. But if I were a member of the family of an MIA and didn't know whether he was dead or alive, I would have a very hard time dealing with that uncertainty.

In 1985 I made *Code of Silence*, which was originally written with Clint Eastwood in mind. Filmed in Chicago, it is the story of Sergeant Eddie Cusack, a second-generation cop who is tough and honest. The enemy in this film is a corrupt and incompetent officer who has burned out and makes it harder and more dangerous for every other cop to do his job. When this officer kills an innocent by-stander, everyone protects him, except for Cusack, who violates the "code of silence" and stands alone in the police force.

I still remember one fight scene that took place on top of a moving elevated train, with people watching from down below. In the middle of a take, a big black woman looked up and shouted, "Chuck, you be careful up there."

New York magazine hailed the film and said, "Norris here takes on Eastwood's patented role of urban avenger—

the cop of 'unorthodox' methods and unlimited daring . . .
Two cheers for Mr. Norris. He might be appalled to find
himself described as a pragmatic liberal, but he's tough
enough to stand anything.''

Code of Silence was my first film to win applause from
the big critics. Vincent Canby of the *New York Times*
called it ''a first-rate action picture. . . . It stands, at long
last, to put Mr. Norris up there with the two other big guys
of Hollywood law and order—Clint Eastwood and Charles
Bronson.''

The praise I remember best came in a letter from Burt
Reynolds, who had screened the picture for some friends
at his home. ''They all loved it,'' he wrote, and added,
''The best compliment I can give you is that I'm extremely
jealous. Just remember, you're only as good as your last
film, so be very careful with what films you pick. Love
and respect, Burt Reynolds.''

It was super to get these kind of accolades, especially
since I also believed that *Code of Silence* was a very good
film. To be honest, I'd have felt terrible if the critics had
knocked me on that picture because, by then, I had been in
the business nine years and I had worked hard at becoming
an actor. Besides getting excellent critical notices, *Code of
Silence* grossed almost eleven million dollars during its
first two weekends. It was number one on the box-office
charts for a month. Thanks to its success I was finally
considered a bankable actor. This meant I could pretty
much pick the films *I* wanted to do.

*   *   *

I was undecided about what my next film project would be until I read an article in a magazine about three terrorist camps headquartered in Iran. Their main goals were espionage and infiltration in the United States and France. One of the groups was also trained for such suicide missions as the incident in Beirut when terrorists attacked a Marine barracks. The article stated that there were hundreds of trained terrorists in America in ''deep cover,'' meaning that they operate as honest citizens for years or even decades until they are called upon to go into action.

I started thinking about the havoc these people could wreak if they organized and started blowing up shopping centers, houses, and public places. The result would be that Americans would be hostages in their own homes. I started to rough out a film idea based on the notion that this could happen in the United States. Threatened to its very foundations by the terrorists, America fights back and overcomes them. That's the American way, and it has been for over two hundred years. Push us and we'll push back.

My original story idea was developed into a screenplay. The movie opens with a boatload of refugees fleeing Castro's Cuba. They are intercepted by a fake Coast Guard cutter under the command of a man named Rostov, who goes aboard to welcome the refugees. Moments later his sailors open fire, slaughtering all the unarmed exiles.

The next sequence shows my character, Matt Hunter, wrestling with an alligator at his Florida retreat. Hunter has retired from the CIA, where he was an antiterrorist

202

specialist. At one time in the past he thwarted Rostov, one of the Soviets' most dangerous and villainous agents.

Rostov is obsessed with a desire for revenge on Hunter, who he feels is the only man who can stop him and his large invasion force of several hundred Communist mercenaries. The CIA suspects that Rostov is in the country and asks Hunter to come out of retirement. He refuses, until his best friend is murdered. Hunter then takes on the assignment but insists that he be allowed to work alone.

The invasion force beaches three landing craft full of Communist mercenaries in an isolated area off the Florida coast. The mercenaries turn their firepower on undefended tract homes, put on police uniforms and slaughter the citizenry, blow up malls, and dynamite churches. Martial law is imposed.

Thanks to some clever media manipulation, Hunter engineers a showdown with Rostov near the top of Atlanta's towering Georgia Pacific skyscraper.

I did more dangerous stunts in *Invasion USA* than in any other film of my career. For example, I spent weeks at an alligator farm in the Everglades learning to wrestle with gators. It was hard and grueling work, but it was an integral facet of the character I was playing, so it had to be done.

I came very close to being seriously injured while filming a climactic scene in which the terrorists attack a shopping mall. That scene alone cost five million dollars to film and required 350 extras playing terrorists. The highlight of it was a sequence in which I come crashing into the mall with my vehicle, then jump out and battle with the terrorists. At the height of the battle, two terrorists jump into a pickup truck and attempt to get away. I was to jump on the side of the truck and fight with the passenger while Don Pike, the stunt driver, powered through the mall. It was a tricky bit of business because Don had to pick a path through the huge beams that held up the ceiling. At the end of the sequence he was to crash through a large plate-glass window. Because the scene was so difficult and expensive, it had to be done on the first take if possible. Aaron told me the stunt was too dangerous for me. I argued with him. I told him that since I would be hanging on to the side of the truck, I could always jump off if the scene got too risky. Aaron insisted it might not be that easy. But I finally convinced him to let me do the stunt myself. It turned out that he was right—it wasn't easy.

When the truck went crashing through the mall with me hanging on, debris was scattered in all directions. Some of the flying debris hit me in the face, causing me to turn my head away. Worse, the debris also hit the windshield, making it difficult for Don to see. As we careened along, Don noticed a beam and swerved at the last second, just barely missing it. The beam creased my back. A few inches closer and I would have been crushed. When the truck finally came to a stop, Aaron came running up, white as a ghost, screaming, "That's it, that's it. I swear I'll never let you do another stunt." He still does, though.

Invasion USA took in over $6.8 million in its first

weekend, one of the biggest opening grosses ever reported for an independent film. It continued to draw moviegoers and became the box-office champion of the 1985 summer season.

I recently learned that of the thousands of films MGM has in their video library, after the all-time best-seller, *Gone with the Wind,* the second best-seller is *Invasion USA,* followed by *The Sound of Music* and *Missing in Action.*

Although some critics are not enthused about my pro-American stance in the films I choose to make, the letters I receive prove to me that a lot of people feel the way I do: it's time for America to strike back.

That was also the theme of my next film, *The Delta Force.* Again, the screenplay was developed from an idea of mine. When the TWA plane was hijacked in Beirut in June 1985, I was glued to the television set watching the news reports. Like everyone else I was concerned about the hostages and hoped that they would be freed unharmed. When the young Navy diver was brutally beaten and then shot to death, I was frustrated and furious, wishing that the Delta Force—the American commandos who were on alert—would go in, resolve the situation, and get revenge. But that never happened.

I had a contract with Cannon to do more films, so I called Menachem Golan, president of the company, and told him that I wanted to make a movie in which the Delta Force did go in and release the captives. I gave him my ideas, and Menachem and Jim Bruner wrote the screenplay.

The first half of the film set the scene as realistically as possible, in keeping with the news reports. It was in the second half that we took liberties and had the Delta Force go in and accomplish what we felt should have been done.

Filmed in Israel, *The Delta Force* had three Academy Award-winners: Lee Marvin, Martin Balsam, and Shelley Winters. My son Eric, who had decided he wanted to be an actor, played a hostage.

Much of this book was written on location in Mexico, where I filmed *Firewalker,* my eighteenth film, an action-comedy with Lou Gossett, Jr. *Firewalker* was a fun film for me because it reveals a lighter side of my character.

I believe that the public wants me to be a free spirit—a man who deals with whatever odds he's given. I think the secret to the success of my movies is that many people want and need someone to identify with, a man who is self-reliant, stands on his own two feet, and is not afraid to face adversity. They want to believe in me, just as I believed in John Wayne when I was a boy. Movies are a way of releasing the youngster in us. Fantasy keeps life going. That may be escapism, but that's what movies are—a way to get away and forget about the problems of everyday life.

I have worked hard these last few years to get my critics to look at me in a different light. It has been a slow process. My image started changing with *Lone Wolf McQuade*, and *Code of Silence* completed the transition. My long-range plan was to break that mold of the "chop-socky" actor by cutting down on the amount of karate I did in my films. I have finally done it! The public has accepted me as an actor who does martial arts rather than a martial artist who acts. I am now known as action star Chuck Norris.

But the martial arts—physically and philosophically—have been the foundation on which I have built my life as a man and film actor.

Whenever I have a film out I prefer to see it in a theater rather than in a private screening because I want to gauge the audience reaction for myself. After all, my movies are made for the public. They're the ones paying the money.

The worst thing I can think of would be to hear someone leaving the theater after seeing one of my movies say, "Boy, was that a ripoff of six bucks." No matter how much work I put into a movie or how favorably the critics view it, I'll be in a world of trouble if it fails at the box office, because then I'll know that the people I made the movie for have not been reached.

You can't sit back and wait for breaks to come your way. They don't happen by hoping: they happen because of positive actions. Maintain a positive attitude about anything you want to achieve, and do what has to be done.

ELEVEN

DURING THE PAST two decades I have done hundreds of interviews, talked with thousands of youngsters in schools, and given advice to countless parents and young people who want to know about my life and karate.

One of the questions most frequently asked of me by parents is: "What real value will my child get from studying karate other than learning how to defend himself?"

The core of martial-arts training is respect and discipline. Respect begins the moment the student enters the studio and bows. It is reflected in the way he treats his instructors as well as the other students. Most important, he learns respect for other authority figures, such as his parents.

Students are expected to conform to certain established

rules of discipline when training. Standards for promotion are generally high and require diligent, repetitive practice and concentration. The incentive system—with graduation to a higher rank as the reward—encourages students to keep training, thus establishing a habit of sticking with something they have started. This discipline invariably aids youngsters with their schoolwork because it facilitates proper habits of study. It also helps them cope with the trials and tribulations of ordinary life.

Martial artists are encouraged to be courteous, patient, and loyal. These are values that are not specifically taught in most Western sports, but they are basic to karate. Values learned in the studio give the student concrete and realistic rules for behavior in his life.

Martial-arts training will also help alleviate the fear most of us have about handling a physical altercation. Before I started studying karate I was insecure about my ability, as a nonfighter, to cope with certain situations. I found that as I gained some proficiency in the martial arts those insecurities diminished. Finally I looked back and wondered why it was important to me that I learn how to fight. I've been in the martial arts for twenty-seven years and I have never had to use my training in a real-life situation, but if I hadn't trained I would have been worrying all these years about what I would do if something did happen. The fact is that when you become capable in any of the arts, problems requiring physical force don't seem to arise, because you are prepared and you reflect this security within yourself.

*   *   *

I am frequently asked what is the best age to start studying a martial art.

Anybody, regardless of age, can study a martial art. Youngsters with proper motivation can start at the age of five; a child may not know his left foot from his right, but he may be very good at emulating what he sees. And I know men and women who started training in their sixties and seventies. What is so great about the martial arts is that they aren't restricted to a specific age. Everything in karate, for instance, is done from a standing position, and kicks and punches are learned without body contact—that way you can maintain or increase your flexibility and coordination at any age.

Adults as well as youngsters often ask me to suggest a particular martial art for them to study.

In my view, all martial-arts systems are sources of education in values because the instructors are usually very specific about the ways students are expected to behave, not only in the studio but in the outside world as well.

There are more than 250 martial-arts styles, and around 7,500 martial-arts studios in the United States that offer instruction. Within that range, there should be a style for everyone, regardless of age, physical condition, or sex. Ten years ago only three percent of karate students were women. Today women make up twenty-five percent of the students.

The first thing I suggest to anyone interested in studying

karate is that he or she take stock of his or her physical condition and limitations. A person who is short and powerfully built with a low center of gravity would do well to investigate judo. Males or females who are already limber or want to become more flexible might find one of the Korean styles—such as tae kwon do or hapkido—of interest. Someone with fast hands and good coordination who is not adverse to a hard workout should look into Japanese karate styles, such as gojo-ryu or shotokan karate. A slightly built person who is not very strong may find jujitsu or aikido appealing because these styles turn an opponent's strength against him. An older person would do well to consider t'ai chi, one of the most ancient of the martial arts, which is still practiced daily by millions of elderly people in China.

Do careful research before choosing a martial art you want to study. You can do this by visiting the public library and reading books that give an overview of the various arts and their history. Or go to your local newsstand and buy some of the martial-arts magazines on sale. Read the articles. Study the pictures. Pick a martial art that appeals to you and find out whether it is being taught in your area. Some of the magazines also include addresses of schools.

What really makes any martial-arts system worthwhile, however, is the instructor. Almost every instructor has credentials that you can verify, but the instructor's rank (from first-degree black belt to, in rare cases, eighth-degree) is not that important. What matters is that you find a man or woman who demonstrates discipline in class and who attempts to bring out the maximum potential in each student. Choose an instructor who is really concerned with his or her students.

Visit two or three schools in your area and ask for permission to watch a class in session. Do this a few times so you can see students of various ranks working out. I would not consider joining a school that would not allow me to watch a training class. You want to know what you are getting into. You also want to find out whether the head instructor himself teaches all the classes or whether he has lower ranks instructing. If you are interested in an Asian style, be certain you can understand the instructor's English.

Watching classes in session will also give you an indication of whether the style has too much—or not enough—physical contact for your taste. If possible, talk with members of the class. This will give you an opportunity to decide whether these are the kind of people you want to spend a few hours with each week.

A follow-up to that is: how long must one study to become proficient in the martial arts?

Karate expertise is not easily or quickly acquired. It is the result of hard training and frequent practice. A minimum of two or three years of three to four classes a week is usually required to achieve some proficiency. I have been studying martial arts for twenty-seven years and I am constantly learning new techniques as well as expanding my abilities by constant daily practice.

*　　*　　*

Another question I am often asked is: "How does karate training relate to daily life?"

If we think of the studio as a microcosm of the world in which we live, then proper karate training can help us discover our weaknesses and strengths. Our lives are composed of a series of engagements and problems to be solved. The solutions learned in the studio can often be applied to life.

For instance, martial-arts training teaches us to avoid confrontations. If our habit or nature is to immediately respond to an attack with a counterattack, this is an area in which we can improve our abilities on the mat as well as our relationships in life. We never meet an attack head-on. There are other alternatives: avoiding it by moving aside; diverting an attacker's energy and force so that it is rendered harmless; turning his force against him; or stepping back and considering the nature of the attack (that is, is it an expression of anger or frustration or just a threat?).

A verbal threat is only that—words. Threats, even insults, are not worthy of a physical response. People who make such threats are usually insecure. A threat of physical violence is generally an attempt by someone to goad another person into an angry response. Training teaches us to control our emotions, to remain calm at all times, to consider alternatives, and to avoid meeting force with force. It also teaches us to control our egos, because we are secure.

Proper training also teaches posture, which, in the Japanese use of the word, is more than just the way you stand or move. It also includes your mental posture—the way you communicate to others, by your attitude, that you are physically and mentally prepared. Your vibes can trigger either negative or positive responses. For example, I have never had to use my martial-arts ability in a confrontation because my body language and my attitude are not threatening.

Recent studies report that muggers and other social predators study potential victims for signs of weakness, generally determined by how they walk and carry themselves. A person who is physically and psychologically centered, who gives off an attitude of awareness and strength, is usually left alone.

Training teaches control. When I was fighting, it was incumbent upon me and my opponent to focus our attacks, to stop short of doing damage. We were responsible for controlling any technique used—just as in an argument, for example, you are responsible for what you say and therefore must learn control.

If you demonstrate lack of control in your personal relationships, there will always be conflict in your life. Mature individuals control their behavior. As a result, others tend to treat them with respect.

Karate students frequently ask me whether I think a top-rank karate fighter could beat a boxer of the same class.

In 1974 a promoter contacted me and asked just that question. I told him it had nothing to do with the style—it depended on the men, since they were both involved in combative arts.

He said he had a proposition for me and asked whether I would like to fight a boxer.

"Whom do you have in mind?" I asked.

"Muhammad Ali," he said.

"Naturally," I said. "You would choose the best."

"We'll pay you a million dollars."

"For a million dollars I'd fight King Kong," I said, figuring that the worst thing Ali could do was knock me out.

The promoter next called Ali to see whether he would agree to the match, for which he was to be paid five million dollars. Ali's wife, who was a black belt in tae kwon do, was listening in on an extension phone. When the conversation ended, she told Ali that I would kick his butt. Whether or not I could have is debatable, because the fight never came off.

I know of several instances in which karate fighters have used their expertise effectively in real confrontations. For example, one of my biggest rivals when I was competing was my good friend Skipper Mullins.

Some time ago Skipper, who was in his mid-twenties but looked like a skinny teenager you could step on like a bug, was staying at my house and decided he wanted to go into town alone for a few beers. Three men in the bar started picking on him. Skipper is happy-go-lucky; he never shows anger. He tried to cool them out, but they persisted. Finally he'd had enough. "OK," he said. "You guys want to fight, let's go outside."

They followed him out, expecting to have a little fun at his expense. The moment they got outside, Skipper spun around and kicked two of them so fast they didn't know what had happened. The third one just stood there dumbfounded, looking down at his friends sprawled on the ground. "Well, come on," Skipper said. The fellow just stood there. "Hell, you don't want to fight," Skipper said, and he went back into the bar. This time no one bothered him.

A television interviewer recently asked me what I would do if I were surrounded by a group of muggers demanding my wallet.

"I'd give it to them," I said.

The interviewer almost dropped the microphone. "You mean to say that you, a karate champion, wouldn't fight?"

"That's right," I said. "If my life or someone else's was in danger, it would be a different story, and I would go all out. But I'm not going to get into a fight over my wallet. I wouldn't want to risk getting injured myself or hurting someone else for anything as insignificant as a few dollars."

Another question, related to the previous one, is: how would a karate practitioner fare against a man with a gun?

The answer varies with the situation. David Glickman, a close friend of mine and one of the top trial attorneys in the country, was asked to defend a man who had come home from work one day and caught his wife in bed with another man. The husband went to a dresser drawer and got out a gun. At that point the lover jumped out of bed and came charging toward him. The husband, who knew that the lover was a black belt in karate, shot and killed him.

David planned his defense along the lines that a black-belt practitioner's karate skill is considered to be a deadly weapon, and the husband had acted in self-defense. David called me and I agreed to be a professional witness for the defense.

On the day of the trial, I was called to the witness stand for cross-examination by the assistant district attorney.

"Do you expect the court to believe that a black belt in karate would have a chance against a man with a gun?" he asked me.

"It's possible," I said. "It would depend on the distance."

"How about ten feet?" the DA asked.

"If the gun was not already cocked and aimed, I believe it is possible."

The attorney asked me to step down from the witness stand and wait in front of the jury. He walked over to the bailiff and asked him to remove the cartridges from his gun and give it to him. The DA joined me in front of the jury with the empty gun in his hand. He made a show of pacing off ten feet and then faced me, saying, "I'd like you to stop me before I can cock and fire the gun."

Holy cow, I thought, What have I gotten myself into? I was wearing a suit with tight-fitting trousers and street shoes.

The DA held the gun at his side and instructed the bailiff to tell us when to begin. The bailiff shouted, "Now."

Before the DA could cock the gun, I had my foot on his chest. I didn't follow through with the kick because I didn't want to hurt him.

The DA was nonplussed. "Let's do it again," he said. "My thumb slipped."

The bailiff gave the word. Once more, I had my foot on the DA's chest before he could cock the gun.

Bob Wall and I then broke some boards to demonstrate the power of karate kicks.

The defendant was acquitted. David told me later that the DA made a bad mistake by asking a question to which he didn't know the answer.

I am most often asked by my contemporaries how I stay in such good shape.

I am now forty-seven years old. I am 5'10" and weigh 170 pounds. My blood pressure is 114/70, and my resting heart rate is 42, the target rate for a distance runner. I am in better physical shape today than I have ever been. I am stronger now than when I was fighting, and my overall conditioning is better. For the first time in my life, thanks to proper and constant exercise, I can do full leg-splits.

I have had to work hard to get limber, and I have to keep at it to stay that way. When I was younger and a competitor I could take a month off from training and then come back to it. I know I can't do that now and maintain a high level of fitness. The human body is like an engine:

keep it finely maintained and tuned and you won't have problems with it, even as far as joints are concerned.

I spend more time each day training than most men can afford to, but since many of my acting roles require that I be in top physical condition, the workouts are really part of my business.

I have a well-equipped gym at my home in Los Angeles, and when I am not in front of the cameras I work out for three hours a day, six days a week. My workout and training partner is Howard Jackson, a former world welterweight kick-boxing champion.

There are many mornings when I don't feel like working out. But I know if I take off one day it will be easier to take the next day off, and eventually I'll stop working out. So I tell myself that maybe the workout won't be as hard today as it was yesterday or as it will be tomorrow, but that I must do something so I don't break the chain of discipline.

The key to my exercise program is its versatility. My normal workout commences daily at 8:00 A.M. On Monday, Wednesday, and Friday I do cardiovascular exercises to develop endurance and heart conditioning. My routine includes karate training—sparring with Howard to increase my speed, focus, and power plus *katas*. I follow my karate workout with an hour of circuit training, which consists of walking on an inclined treadmill, running on a level treadmill, pedaling the Lifecycle, the Turbo 2000, another type of stationary cycle, and concluding with a workout on the rowing machine.

On Tuesday, Thursday, and Saturday I work with weights and do pull-ups, push-ups, and stomach-strengthening exercises on the Total Gym, an all-purpose machine for overall strength training. I frequently work out and train with Lou Ferrigno or Benny Podda, both body-building experts.

When I go on location for a film I usually take along certain equipment, including the Total Gym. I try to get in at least an hour of conditioning a day.

I don't believe in dieting, which is, to me, a negative concept that means doing without. I have never needed the services of a professional dietician because the key to my eating habits has always been moderation. I never over-indulge: I leave the table satisfied but not full. I rarely eat anything that is fried, and I avoid beef. But I do try to eat a lot of turkey, chicken, fish, fruit, and pasta, with the emphasis on high complex carbohydrates. I have only one weakness where sweets are concerned: I love Snickers and always have a bag of the bite-sized bars at hand.

Young competitors at tournaments constantly ask for my "secrets" of winning.

That question reminds me of the gumball machines that proliferated during my childhood. When you put a penny in the machine you got a gumball and a slip of paper with a tersely worded message similar to those that come today in fortune cookies. The fact is, there is no simple answer to the question and no shortcuts. Over the years, however, I have learned that there are many facets to winning, both on and off the mat.

Be in the best possible physical shape.

When I was fighting, I made a point of being in the best possible physical shape before getting into the ring. A trained *karateka* comes onto the mat with a calm and measured tread, in the peak of condition, physically prepared to go the distance and extend himself if necessary.

Learn success imagery.

If you think of yourself as being successful, on the mat as well as in life, you will spark the powerful subconscious into action, and it will work to make the image a reality.

You can win.

I never went into a fight thinking, Oh, gee, I have to fight Joe Lewis [or Skipper Mullins, or Bill Wallace]. If I had allowed that negative thinking, the thought would have been ingrained in my mind. I knew I could not have a defeatist attitude, so I always went into a fight believing that I was going to win.

Control your breathing.

Professional athletes have recently discovered that the way to control anxiety and pressure is to control their breathing. Arthur Ashe and Yannick Noah are two tennis professionals who have learned to overcome "choking" in crucial matches by mastering breath control. Martial artists have known this for centuries, thanks to Zen practices.

The proper way to breathe is to gently take air in through the nose and exhale softly through the mouth.

Breathe regularly at all times. All too often, when you feel under pressure, you neglect to breathe and instead hold air in, gulping away sporadically, only to suffer tight muscles and early fatigue.

Eliminate stress.

Stress is a negative reaction to a tense situation and usually occurs when you are unprepared to deal with whatever you are facing. When I entered a competition I never felt stress because I was physically, psychologically, and mentally prepared.

To eliminate stress from your consciousness you must be prepared to handle any contingency that may arise. You should concentrate on the task at hand and visualize the result you want to achieve. When your mind is focused on that positive result there will be no room for stress.

Turn negatives into positives.

I made many mistakes during my fighting career and lost some matches. When I lost, it was a surprise to me. Later I would sit down and analyze why I had been defeated. I tried to determine what I had done wrong. Then I would train and study so I wouldn't lose the same way again. As a result, I never really felt as though I had lost.

Man can be defeated but not destroyed.

It was Ernest Hemingway who said that. I believe he meant that a defeat was simply that—it was not the end of the world. In my own case, I turned each defeat to my advantage by examining how and why I had lost and determining that I would never be defeated the same way again.

Strive for realistic objectives.

Don't make impossible demands of yourself. My wife, Dianne, is a case in point. She was only a blue belt, but she thought she could win a black-belt tournament even though she didn't have the proper background and training in competition.

Dianne had psyched herself up and visualized herself as a winner, but she was not physically prepared to achieve her goal.

Screen out peripheral thoughts.

Concentrate on what you are doing, not on your opponent. When I was fighting my immediate concern was to land the blow. If it was blocked, then I would react in another way. In tennis they say, "Play the ball and not your opponent." In essence, that means that you should concentrate on making the best shot you can.

Do your homework.

Before each tournament I constantly practiced all my moves and techniques. When I got to the tournament I would study the other fighters. By the time I stepped into the ring I was prepared for almost any eventuality because I had done my homework.

Look for openings to penetrate your opponent's defenses.

An opening can also be a momentary break in concentration. For example, when I was fighting, I made it a practice to study my opponent's pattern of breathing because I know that someone is weaker when inhaling than when exhaling. For a fraction of a second, someone who is breathing in is at a disadvantage because he cannot attack. He must breathe in and then move on the exhalation. So I would time my own onslaught for when I saw him inhaling. Bruce Lee was a master of this technique; he invariably timed his moves for when his opponent was least expecting them.

Keep your cool.

Through training we learn that anger is self-defeating. An angry fighter is careless: he wants to hurt his opponent; he ceases to think as a human being and responds as an animal; he loses control of himself and the situation.

During the last two decades I have spoken on a volunteer basis with thousands of underprivileged youngsters. They most often ask me what my personal philosophy is.

A simple answer is: "Think positively." I believe there are two distinct paths we can follow in life: positive and negative. On the positive path, you don't wait for things to happen—you *make* them happen by setting goals and working hard to achieve them, no matter how long it takes.

On the negative path, you feel that you don't have a choice, that nothing good will come to you in your life, that you are foredoomed. If you say to yourself, I can't do this or that, *can't* becomes the operative word in your vocabulary and results in self-fulfilling failure. The person who says *I can* has already started on the path toward success.

You must be positive about everything you do because it is easy to be affected by negative thinking. All you need do is listen to the people around you. There will always be someone who tells you that you can't achieve something you want because you are not big enough, not small enough, not dark enough, not light enough, not qualified enough, or too qualified. The people who tell you this are frequently not successful themselves.

When I wanted to get into films, I was constantly told that action films were on the decline; no one was interested in me because everyone considered me an athlete. If I had accepted such judgments I would never have persisted. I treated the initial rejections as only temporary because I knew that with enough time, determination, and hard work, as well as a positive mental attitude, I could succeed.

Developing a positive mental attitude requires training. The human will becomes stronger each time it is used. If a man were to do five push-ups every day for one week, the following week he would be able to do six push-ups a day. With each push-up, his arms and chest would become stronger. Like the body, a positive mental attitude can be developed.

When the great boxing champion Gene Tunney was a boy he tested himself constantly. He often went without a

226

favorite dessert while the rest of his family enjoyed the treat; he memorized parts of books to discipline his mind. Later he forced himself to run ten extra steps after his scheduled roadwork. All of this fired his will and determination. As a boxer, he twice defeated one of the most feared heavyweight fighters in history. During his second fight with Jack Dempsey, Tunney was knocked down to the canvas. Most men would have gone down and stayed down. But Tunney's will and positive attitude had been developed through years of training. After a long count, he got up and won the match.

A serious problem facing youngsters today is that too many of them expect such things as wealth and prestige to be handed to them. Everything has its price, and hard work is the norm rather than the exception.

I believe there is too much permissiveness in the home, the school system, and society as a whole today. Many children grow up without discipline. If something doesn't come easily to them they frequently go on to something else without finishing what they have started, thus establishing a bad pattern. I consider it important that once you make up your mind to do something you finish it. It's easy to stop and give up, and then it becomes easier to give up the next time you are faced with something that does not come easily. But each time you finish, your discipline becomes stronger and you gain self-esteem. You feel better within yourself and want to taste that feeling of accomplishment again.

Kids growing up in this country today, whether they

realize it or not, have a great deal to begin with, compared to youngsters in any other country. If you have everything to start with, you frequently don't have the drive to succeed. The important thing, whether you are rich or poor, is deciding what to do with your life and then doing it.

I tell youngsters that despite the fact that I started with nothing, I have reached a substantial level of success in my life. I matured from a shy, insecure nonachiever to a confident person who has achieved personal and professional success. As a result of my own experience, I believe that anyone can overcome his handicaps and accomplish anything he wants. It's still possible in America to start at the bottom of the pile and climb the ladder of success IF you have the determination to stick with it and not let any obstacles keep you from reaching whatever goal you have set for yourself.

Very few people become successful overnight at any endeavor. Most successful people have learned to stick with whatever it is they wish to achieve and to move step by step until they reach their objective.

To me, the exciting thing about life is overcoming the obstacles in the way of your goal. When there's a barrier to hurdle, you work, work, and work until you finally get over that barrier. Then you say to yourself, Wow, that was tough, but I did it. Achieving something difficult builds inner strength and encourages you to go on to your next goal.

Once you achieve your goal you will have to find something else to reach for, because if you don't, life will lose its meaning. I believe that you must always have something to keep you motivated in order to get up in the morning.

I know many successful people, and one common denominator is their refusal to ever be completely satisfied. They keep pushing forward, exploring new avenues, reaching for new challenges.

The secret of inner strength is in practice—yesterday, today, tomorrow. Today I have more than I ever dreamed possible: a loving family, a successful career, happiness, and peace of mind. But I know that when I reach one goal I must find another, and I must always strive toward new horizons. I have no idea what the future holds in store for me, but I look forward to it with optimism.

By accomplishing what is difficult, we make the concept of success part of our lives. Failure does not exist—what is considered failure is merely a chance to learn and prepare for success.

Man can be defeated but not destroyed. A defeat is simply that, and not the end of the world. Treat defeat as a temporary setback. Learn from it and try again with renewed vigor and determination.

There is no finish line. When you reach one goal, find a new one. Always reach for new horizons.

My Principles Of Inner Strength

BASED UPON MY own life experiences, I have formulated some principles of inner strength that have worked for me. They are sorted into three categories: principles to help you achieve your personal goals, principles to improve your relationships with the world at large, and principles to enhance your life.

How to Achieve Your Personal Goals

Use positive imagery. The first thing to do if you want to improve any area of your life is to establish the goal in your mind and form a mental picture of it. Visualize yourself successfully achieving the goal, and always keep that mental image. Determination and persistence will usually overcome all the obstacles in your way if you train and mentally prepare yourself properly.

If the goal seems distant and impossible, chart the path to it into small steps and take each step one at a time. Do what is necessary but remain open to change or chance along the way. What seems to be a detour may often turn out to be fortuitous.

Control your own destiny. You can do this at any time by planting the proper seed. If you feed and nourish it, sooner or later it will bear fruit.

Everything you do should be a stepping-stone toward making your personal dream a reality. But you can't sit back waiting for the breaks to come your way. They don't happen by hoping; they happen by positive actions. If you feel deep in your heart that you can accomplish something—no matter how impossible it seems—and if you are determined and persistent enough, you can succeed. But always remember that there is no finish line. When you reach one goal, find another. Always reach for new horizons.

Take a chance. There is truth to that old adage, "Nothing ventured, nothing gained." If you don't get into the game, you can't play or win. If you do something you have previously been afraid to try, you will crack the egg of your insecurity. You can always do a little more than you thought you could if you push yourself beyond your limitations. Accomplishing something difficult gives you the strength to go on to further success.

Failure is only a matter of interpretation. The only time you really fail is when you don't learn from the experience. Say to yourself, I'll never lose that way again. A true champion or winner can deal with his failures as well as his successes and can learn from both. But if you do lose, remember that one of the keys to inner strength is accepting the inevitable with grace and style.

Accept help. My lesson in life has been learning to listen. Almost everyone has something of value to teach you. You can learn about life from the most unexpected sources, even children. It's a wise man who goes to others for help. Everyone was a beginner at some point in his life; even our teachers were once pupils.

Learn to trust your subconscious. Never think to yourself, I can't do this. Negative attitudes yield negative emotions, just as positive attitudes encourage positive emotions. Your subconscious mind takes you at your word, and you won't be able to succeed. Think positively, and your subconscious will help you achieve your desires by giving your conscious mind a new blueprint. You can even trust your subconscious to solve problems for you while you are asleep. The subconscious never rests and is always working.

233

Think of yourself as a leader rather than a follower. Your subconscious will take it for a fact, and you will act accordingly.

Be prepared. Remember that he who fails to prepare prepares to fail. A loser says to himself, If I win . . .; a winner says to himself, When I win. . . . You must prepare physically, mentally, and psychologically to achieve your goal. Preparation in just one of these areas is not enough.

Always remember that you are unique. If you compare yourself to your competition, you allow yourself to be intimidated in advance because you subconsciously place yourself below that person and your subconscious mind will take it as a fact. Surpassing another person should never be your goal; the only thing that matters is what you accomplish yourself.

How to Get Along Better with Others

Like yourself. If you like yourself you are more likely to feel good about other people, and they will respond to you positively. When you have an enthusiasm about life you will attract people with the same passion.

Be open-minded. Only when we learn not to judge others but rather to totally accept and not want to change them can we learn to accept ourselves.

Avoid confrontations. If you get to the point where you have to fight, you've already lost the battle. With nothing to prove, there is no need for a confrontation. Try self-effacing humor to defuse an unpleasant encounter.

Never underestimate an opponent. Overconfidence in your own ability is a mistake because when you're over-confident you don't mentally prepare for whatever it is you intend to do. You can be defeated as easily by overconfi-dence on your part as by another person's skill.

Make friends. It's just as easy to make a friend as it is to make an enemy. You generally get back what you give out in a first meeting. Smile, and you can expect a smile in return. If you are hostile you can anticipate a hostile response. Something as casual as a meeting with a stranger can often change the course of your life. Be open to new opportunities to make friends.

Keep friends. Cherish and nourish your friendships. Friends can be your strongest personal support system in difficult times. When you are angry with a friend, consider the good times shared and ask yourself whether they bal-ance out the hard times. If they do, don't end the friendship. Don't condemn people for what they are; either accept them or avoid them.

Never be ashamed to say "I love you." Those three words that mean so much are not said often enough.

How to Make Your Life Better

Make the best of every day. When things seem to be at their worst, look around and see the problems other people face—they will probably make yours seem minuscule. As bad as things seem to be, always remember that there are people worse off than you are.

The center of your life should be living. Appreciate every moment of life that God allows you, because life is fragile. Do not sacrifice today for a tomorrow that may never come or for a yesterday that is gone. Learn from yesterday and live for today. While you are living and striving, do it to the fullest because today will soon become yesterday, and you won't have the opportunity to experience this moment again.

Chuck Norris's Code of Ethics

I will develop myself to the maximum of my potential in all ways.

I will forget the mistakes of the past and press on to greater achievements.

I will always be in a positive frame of mind and convey this feeling to every person I meet.

I will continually work at developing love, happiness, and loyalty in my family and acknowledge that no other success can compensate for failure in the home.

I will look for the good in all people and make them feel worthwhile.

If I have nothing good to say about a person, I will say nothing.

I will give so much time to the improvement of myself that I will have no time to criticize others.

I will always be as enthusiastic about the success of others as I am about my own.

I will maintain an attitude of open-mindedness toward another person's viewpoint while still holding fast to what I know to be true and honest.

I will maintain respect for those in authority and demonstrate this respect at all times.

I will always remain loyal to my country and obey the laws of the land.

I will remain highly goal-oriented throughout my life because that positive attitude helps myself, my family, and my country.

Chuck Norris Tournament History

1965 Los Angeles All-Star Championships
   Grand Champion

   California State Championships
   Grand Champion

   Winter Nationals (San Jose)
   Grand Champion

1966 International Karate Championships (Long Beach)
   Middleweight Champion

   National Winter Karate Championships (San Jose)
   Grand Champion

   International Karate Federation Championships
   First Place

1967 North America Championships (New York)
    Grand Champion

    All-American Championships (New York)
        Grand Champion

    National Tournament of Champions (Cleveland)
        Grand Champion

    American Tang Soo Do Championships (Washington, D.C.)
        Grand Champion

    Central Valley Championships (Stockton California)
        Grand Champion

    International Karate Championships (Long Beach)
        Middleweight Champion
        Grand Champion
        Korean-Style Kata Champion

    Tournament of Champions (New York)
        Grand Champion

    All-American Open Karate Championships (New York)
        Lightweight Champion
        Grand Champion

    International Karate Championships (Long Beach)
        Grand Champion

1968 U.S. Championships (Dallas)
    Lightweight Champion

    All-American Karate Championships (New York)
        Grand Champion

    Long Beach Internationals
        Grand Champion

    World Professional Karate Championships (New York)
        Middleweight Champion

Second American Tang Soo Do Invitational (Washington, D.C.)
> *Grand Champion*

Hawaii-U.S. Mainland Competition (Honolulu)
> *member of winning team*

East Coast vs. West Coast Karate Championships (New York)
> *member of West Coast team*

1969 World Professional Karate Championships (New York)
> *Middleweight Champion*

International Karate Championships (Long Beach)
> *Korean-Style Kata Champion*

Note: From 1967 to 1969, Chuck Norris's Black Belt Karate Team went undefeated in eighty straight matches.

1970 U.S. Team Championships (Long Beach, California)
> *member of winning team*

241

Chuck Norris
Films

The Wrecking Crew, 1968
Directed by Phil Karlson
Role: bodyguard

Return of the Dragon, 1973
Directed by Bruce Lee
Role: Bruce Lee's adversary

Breaker! Breaker!, 1977
Directed by Don Hulette
Role: truck driver John David Dawes

Good Guys Wear Black, 1977
Directed by Ted Post
Role: Professor John T. Booker

A Force of One, 1979
Directed by Paul Aaron
Role: Matt Logan

The Octagon, 1980
Directed by Eric Karson
Role: Scott James

An Eye for an Eye, 1981
Directed by Steve Carver
Role: Detective Sean Cain

Silent Rage, 1982
Directed by Michael Miller
Role: Sheriff Dan Stevens

Forced Vengeance, 1982
Directed by James Fargo
Role: Josh Randall

Lone Wolf McQuade, 1982
Directed by Steve Carver
Role: Texas Ranger James J. McQuade

Missing in Action, 1984
Directed by Joseph Zito
Role: Colonel James Braddock

Missing in Action 2: The Beginning, 1985
Directed by Lance Hool
Role: Colonel James Braddock

Code of Silence, 1985
Directed by Andy Davis
Role: Sergeant Eddie Cusack

Invasion U.S.A., 1985
Directed by Joseph Zito
Screenplay by James Bruner and Chuck Norris
Role: Matt Hunter

The Delta Force, 1986
Directed by Menachem Golan
Role: Scott McCoy

Firewalker, 1987
Directed by J. Lee Thompson
Role: Max Donigan

Braddock: Missing in Action 3, 1987
Directed by Aaron Norris
Role: Colonel James Braddock

New York Times bestsellers—
Books at their best!

Bestselling Thrillers —
action-packed for a great read